Acknowledgements

The authors very much a[ppreciate ...] ing the research into the histor[y ...] Norman Brown, Clare Church, El[... ...] Irwin, Margaret Tatler and Alex Worswick.

They are very grateful to relatives of occupants who provided much personal information, namely Peter and Tony Cole for Constance Elizabeth Bairstow; Sarah Horn (nee East) for Charles Harry East and family; Angela Martell for Esme Noble nee Willetts and Anna Pugh and her cousin Gill for information about Annie Millicent Comont nee Boulton.

Particular thanks are given to Ann Noble, nee Burcher, granddaughter of William and Esme Noble, and her Uncle John who gave their personal memories of them and their life at The Clans; also to Joyce Sutcliffe (formerly Howard) who was the last person to run the house as a hotel.

The authors are indebted to John & Carol Hutber for giving access to the original parchment documents that they have relating to St. Ronan's. These gave much valuable information, particularly since no documents relating to No. 34 prior to 1998 can be found. Thanks are also due to Tom Barter for his assistance in communication with the Land Registry in regard to the search for original documentation.

The authors acknowledge permission to reproduce maps and other material provided by the British Library, Malvern Hills Conservators, Malvern Hills District Council, Malvern Hills Town Council, Malvern Museum, Malvern Library and the Ordnance Survey Commission.

Valuable assistance was also received from staff at The Malvern Museum, Malvern Conservators, Malvern Library and Malvern Council, particularly Lyndsey Davies and others for their help in locating graves within Malvern Town Cemetery. Similar information for St. James' Cemetery was provided by Rev. David Nicholls and for Malvern Wells by David Taverner, Parish Clerk.

Contents

	Page
Acknowledgements	iii
Summary	viii
List of Illustrations	x

1 Land and Original Building

1.1	Southfield Area		1
1.2	34 Priory Road, Malvern, Worcestershire		13

2 Family Histories for Main Owners or Occupiers c.1855 to 1985

2.1	Edward Ratheram	Jun 1855 to 1871	27
2.2	Harriet Frances Ratheram	Feb 1871	45
2.3	Thomas Lane	Mar to Aug 1871	48
2.4	Hon. John Henry Roper - Curzon	Aug 1871 to Apr 1886	50
2.5	Harriet Ann Roper Curzon nee Brown	Apr 1886 to Sep 1888	57
2.6	Major General Henry Imlach Bett	Apr 1890 to Jun 1894	60
2.7	Dr. Charles Harry Hanger East	Oct 1894 to 1921	67
2.8	Dr. John Henry Dixon Phelps	1922 to 1934	78
2.9	Constance Elizabeth Bairstow nee Hiley	1937 to 1941	87
2.10	Admiralty WRNS Hostel	1941 to 1945	99
2.11	Griffith Rowland Owen,	1948	101

v

		Laura Margaret Owen nee Jones		
	2.12	William Noble, Esme Noble nee Willetts	1950 to 1964	106
	2.13	Electoral Register Entries	1964 to 1968	121
	2.14	Annie Millicent Comont, formerly Serjent, nee Boulton	1968 to 1969	122
	2.15	Joyce Margaret Howard, nee Webster	1969 to 1972	129
	2.16	Dennis Harold Tatler, Margaret Shirley Tatler	1972 to 1985	137

3 Planning Applications after 1985

    3.1   Miss C. Ward   140
    3.2   Limbrick Developments Ltd.   140
    3.3   Bovis Homes   141

4 Priory Gardens

    4.1   Construction   145
    4.2   Purchase Of The Freehold   147

Appendices	Page
A1 Names of Adjacent Properties in Priory Road	148

A2 Malvern Cemeteries

A2.1	Great Malvern Cemetery, Madresfield Road, Great Malvern	149
A2.2	Malvern Wells Cemetery, Green Lane, Malvern Wells	152
A2.3	St James' Church Cemetery, West Malvern Road, West Malvern	153

A3 Sources of Information	155
A4 Local Newspapers	161
A5 Trade Directories for Worcester and Malvern	163
Index	165

Summary

This is a record of research undertaken by the authors throughout 2011 - 2012 into the history of the site located at 34 Priory Road, Malvern, WR14 3DR. It includes a brief history of the land before it became available for building and the subsequent buildings that have occupied the site.

The first building was known as Thorpe House (c.1853), St. Clare (1855), St. David's Hotel, (1948) The Clans Private Hotel (1950), Hotel St. Clare (1967) and finally Tower House (1972) until it was demolished in November 1988.

In addition to a description of the building, family histories are recorded for the main owners or occupiers. These include Edward Ratheram (1855), Harriet Ratheram (Jan 1871), Thomas Lane (Feb 1871). the Hon. John Henry Roper-Curzon (Aug 1871), Harriet Ann Roper-Curzon (Apr 1886), Maj. Gen. Henry Imlach Bett (Jul 1890), Dr. Charles Harry Hanger East (Oct 1894), Dr. John Henry D. Phelps (1922), Constance Elizabeth Bairstow (1937), the Admiralty (1941), Griffith Roland Owen and Laura Margaret Owen (1948), William Noble and Esme Noble (1950), Annie Millicent Comont (1968), Joyce M. Howard (1969), Dennis Harold Tatler and Margaret S. Tatler (1972).

There are several periods when the building was apparently unoccupied, namely 1935 to 1937; 1945 to 1947 and 1949 to 1950.

Details are given of a number of planning proposals made for the building and for the site after 1985 and before Priory Gardens was built, commencing in 1999.

The second building, Priory Gardens, is a condominium of 15 flats. All owners are shareholders of Priory Gardens (Malvern) Ltd., the company set up to purchase the freehold and maintain the property.

With the exception of information provided by, and with the agreement of, individual contributors all other information has been obtained from public domain sources.

List of Illustrations

Fig.		Page
1	Malvern in 1744	2
2	Malvern in 1812 from OSD 216	3
3	Malvern in 1827	4
4	Southfields Area of Malvern in 1854	6
5	Drawing from Map of 1884	8
6	Map of St. Clare, 1886	9
7	Map of 1884 revised 1903	10
8	Map of 1884 revised 1938	12
9	The Clans Private Hotel c. 1950	15
10	Plan of Ground Floor of the Building	16
11	Plan of the Site in 1982	18
12	Front view of The Clans Hotel	20
13	Fireplace beneath Lounge Window	22
14	Tomb of Edward and Harriet Ratheram, Malvern Cemetery	44
15	The Inscription on the Tomb of Edward and Harriet Ratheram	44
16	The Burial Plot of the Roper-Curzon family, Malvern Cemetery	56
17	The Inscription for Harriet Ann Roper-Curzon	59
18	The Inscription on the Grave Surround	59
19	The Burial Plot of the East family, Malvern Cemetery	73
20	The Inscription for the East family	73
21	The Burial Plot of the Phelps family, St James' Cemetery, West Malvern	85
22	The inscription for John Henry Phelps	86
23	The inscription for Lucy Olive Phelps	86
24	Constance Elizabeth Bairstow nee Hiley	98
25	An Older Constance Elizabeth Bairstow	98
26	William Noble	118
27	Esme Noble in the Garden of The Clans Hotel	118
28	Margaret Burcher nee Noble and Audrey Evelyn Noble	119
29	The Headstone for the Noble family, Malvern Wells Cemetery	120
30	The Headstone for the Burcher family, Malvern	120

	Wells Cemetery	
31	James Geoffrey Comont and Annie about 1935	127
32	Annie Millicent Comont nee Boulton about 1968	127
33	The Headstone for Annie Millicent Comont in Malvern Cemetery	128
34	Information Card for Hotel St. Clare about 1969	136
35	Tower House drawn by Margaret Tatler 1972	137
36	Tower House Shortly Before Demolition	144
37	Winstanley at the Time of Demolition	144
38	Priory Gardens Site at the Start of Construction	145
39	Priory Gardens, 2001	146
40	Plan of Malvern Town Cemetery	151
41	Plan of Malvern Wells Cemetery	152
42	Plan of St James' Church, Cemetery, West Malvern	154

1. The Land and Original Building

1.1 Southfield Area

The land currently occupied by Priory Gardens, 34 Priory Road, Malvern, Worcestershire, was originally part of the demesne associated with the Benedictine Priory of Much Malvern; Malvern was a small village with a cluster of dwellings at that time. The land consisted mainly of fields, orchards and farmlands situated to the south of the Priory buildings. Following the Dissolution of the Monasteries between 1536 and 1541 this whole area passed into private hands.

In 1541 a 21 year lease was granted to Richard Berde (or Beard) who transferred it to William Pinnock. He then bought the land on the 26th of August 1544 for £140 16s 6d (about £500,000 at 2012 values) and he sold out to John Knottesford on the 19th of May 1545.

In 1580 he settled the property on his eldest daughter Ann Knottesford, who married William Savage of Elmley Castle; for the next two centuries it was passed through their male descendants, together with Elmley Castle, to Thomas Byrche Savage who sold it to James Oliver, a Worcester grocer, in 1744.

Fig. 1 is a map drawn in 1744 by John Doharty at the request of Lord Foley. The location of the original drawings has not been found and Brian Smith in 'The History of Malvern' records that they were no longer in the possession the Foley Estate when that book was written in 1964. There is however a framed copy in Malvern Library.

Fig. 1 Malvern In 1744. Original drawn by John Doharty in 1744 for Lord Foley. Copy made by A. Fraser 1912 held by Malvern Library.

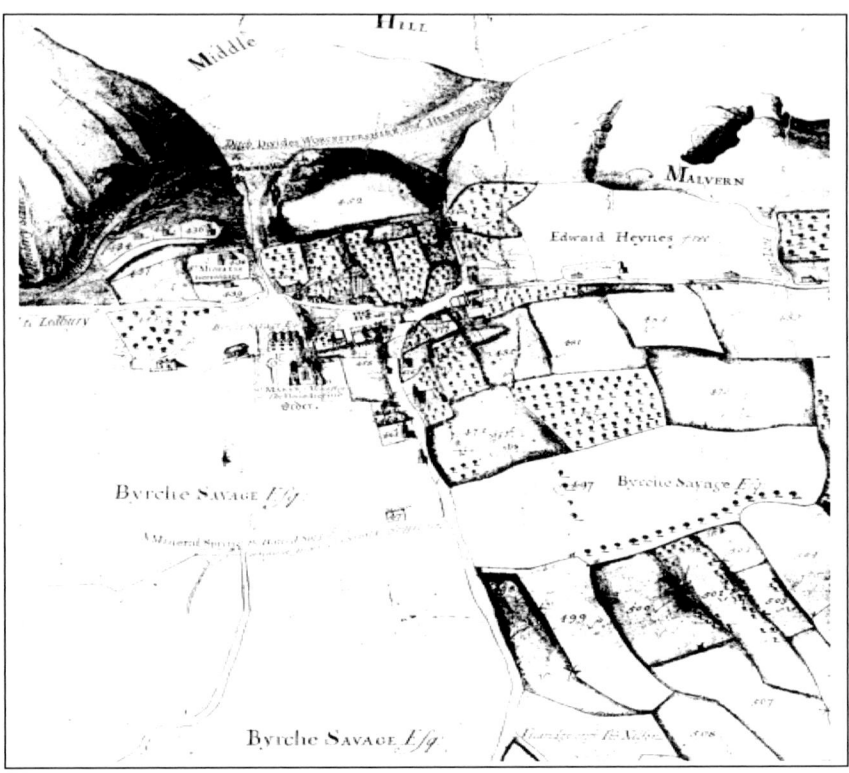

In 1782 the land passed to the Mason family, who were merchants from Birmingham, as part of a marriage settlement between William Wallis Mason and Elizabeth Oliver, daughter of James. This family became very influential and one of the largest land holders in this area of Malvern.

Following the death of William in 1805 various members of the family including Samuel, Mary, James, Philip and Oliver Mason, were involved in ownership of the land. It still consisted mainly of fields associated with Nether Court farmhouse that stood where the Council House now stands.

Fig. 2 Malvern In 1812 From The First Ordnance Survey Drawing Reference OSD216.

Fig. 3 shows the area in 1827 and gives clear indication of the land in the Southfields area of Malvern in the ownership of the Mason Estate. Abbey Road had not been cut through and the main development of the town can be seen to be taking place on Belle Vue Terrace and Worcester Road to the North of Church Street and the Priory.

Fig. 3 Malvern in 1827 original drawn by C. H. Crisp in 1827/1828. Copy by L. F. Baker in 1920 held by Malvern Library. Ref 912.4247.

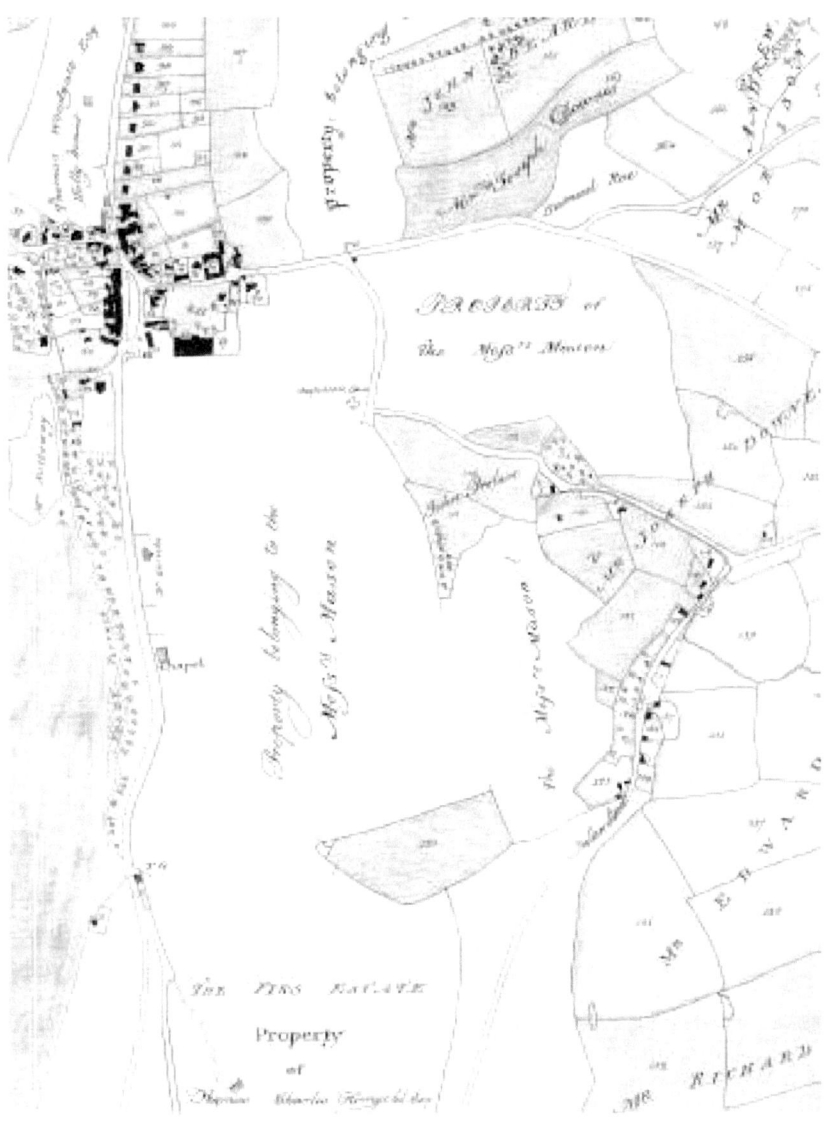

The death of James Mason in London on the 26th of July 1842 prompted the breaking up of the estate and the land was divided into building lots which were offered for sale by auction by Messrs Hobbs and Sons on the 22nd of October 1846, on the instruction of his trustees.

An announcement of the sale in the Worcester Chronicle dated the 21st of October 1846 lists 'Lots 1-14' as being the 'delightful, tithe free land called Southfield' and also included 'a coppice'; a total of about 23 acres. It refers to its proximity to 'the proposed Abbey Road and other roads' and describes the land as suitable for 'Villas and Residences'. It does not distinguish between the lots but they are said to vary in size from about three quarters of an acre to almost three acres.

This differs from land sold by Lady Emily Foley who considered sites should be of about one acre each, but it is understood that both the Mason family and Lady Foley had similar rules that were to be followed by builders of dwellings, including no house to be built immediately opposite nor in line with another and a requirement for the planting of trees to soften the development.

At this time Mill Lane leading from Church Street to the Chalybeate Spring, also known as 'Dog Well', still came only as far as Spa Cottage, built about 1840 as a well house, which today stands alongside the footpath between Priory Road and Orchard Road. It then turned sharply left down to the Corn Mill situated in what is now known as Clarence Road. In the 1500s the lane to the Chalybeate Spring was recorded as 'Piggestye Way'

As building proceeded in the area, Southfields Road was cut through from Abbey Road and Mill Lane was extended beyond Spa Villa to join up with it, eventually becoming known as Priory Road. The surface of the roads at the time, and right up to the beginning of the 20th Century, would have been beaten earth.

Fig. 4 The Southfields Area Of Malvern In 1854. Map Held by Malvern Conservators

The 1850's were a period of rapid development in Malvern. In 1842 Dr James Wilson and Dr James Manby Gully opened Water Cure

Clinics at Malvern which were very popular and were the beginning of the town's prosperity. Many well-known people are recorded as having taken the 'Cure'.

A requirement stipulated by the Mason estate that properties should be for private family use only was subsequently ignored and many houses were used as 'Lodging Houses' to cater for the increasing number of visitors.

A rail link between Worcester and Hereford was first considered in the 1850's when the need to link the Black Country industries with the South Wales coal fields was realised. Work started in 1856 and the line reached Great Malvern in July 1859 and Hereford in September 1861.

Great Malvern Railway Station was opened by Worcester and Hereford Railway in May 1860, the current building, designed by E. W. Elmslie, being completed in 1862. Thus Malvern became easily accessible to the industrial Midlands.

Building in the area continued and in the 1884 Ordnance Survey map, 6 inches to the mile, part of the current Priory Road is shown as Southfields Road although it is referred to in the Malvern Advertiser as Priory Road from April 1872. In the revised edition dated 1903 of the area surveyed in 1884, it is all shown as Priory Road.

Fig. 5 Drawing taken from Map of 1884 held at Malvern Museum

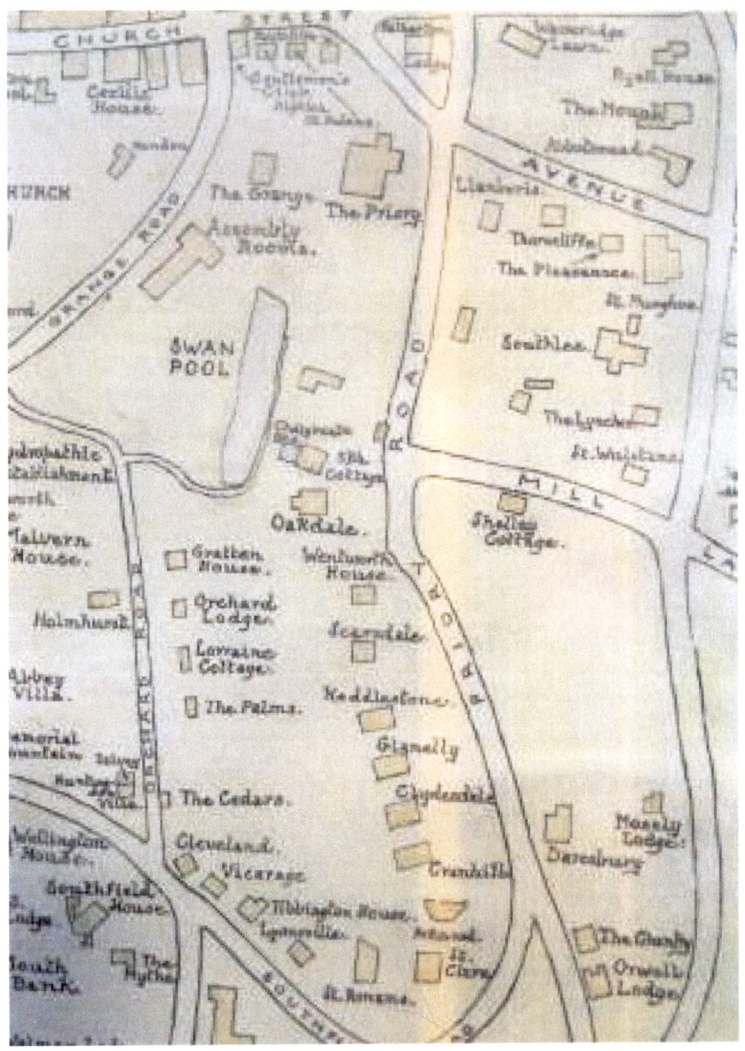

Fig. 6 Map of St Clare 1886 held at Malvern Museum

Fig. 7 Map of 1884 Revised 1903

The name Priory Gardens was first used for the area now known as Priory Park; Malvern Hills District Council website records the history of this area.

In order to cater for the increasing number of visitors to the town entertainment facilities were developed such as Cecilia Hall, Church Street, built in the 1850's and the Royal Spa Concert Hall in 1883. These facilities were superseded in 1885 by the Assembly Rooms and Winter Gardens, now the Theatre complex, in Grange Road.

The building now used as The Council House stands on the site of 'The Priory', the home of Dr. James Manby Gully and he extended the property in 1851 by purchasing the land now occupied by The Splash Leisure Centre. At that time it cost him £700 (£77,000 at 2012 values) and included the walk way between Priory Road and Orchard Road. He built a baths complex on part of the site and used the rest as kitchen gardens.

When Gully left Malvern in 1872 Alfred Speer bought, and immediately demolished, 'The Priory' replacing it with 'Priory Mansion', the current Council House; the building was completed in 1877. He increased the garden of Priory Mansion when he purchased Swan Pool and the grounds associated with the Winter Gardens at auction for £4,500 (£450,000 at 2012 values); in 1888 the buildings were also transferred to him by Malvern Assembly Rooms and Pleasure Gardens Ltd.

Following the death of Alfred Speer in 1894 Priory Mansion was used as a school until it became the Council House in 1925. The 8 acre gardens surrounding Priory Mansion are clearly labelled as 'Priory Gardens' on the 1938 revision of the 1884 Ordnance Survey map (Fig. 8) and the current layout of Priory Park is still very much the same as it is shown on that map.

Fig. 8 Map of 1884 revised 1938

1.2   34 Priory Road, Malvern, Worcestershire

The site area is 0.3 Hectares (0.74 acres). Google Earth gives the location as 52/06/24.78 N., 2/19/20.20 W., and altitude 109m (350 feet).

The first building was originally known as Thorpe House and recorded as occupied in the first edition of the Malvern Advertiser published on the 16th. of June 1855; it was re-named St. Clare in July 1856. The census taken on the 7th of April 1861 includes records for the residents of Portswood, St. Clare, St. Ronan's and Chalford.

The name 'St. Clare' can be seen engraved in the left hand pillar of the stone gate pillars at the east end of the frontage and had been skimmed with cement to hide it but recent, much needed, stabilisation work has removed this infill and the letters 'C L A' can be clearly seen. The engraving is rectangular in cross section and deeper than engraved lettering suggesting it may originally have been inlaid brass.

It was later known as St. David's Hotel from 1948, The Clans Hotel from 1950, the Hotel St. Clare from 1968 and then Tower House, probably from about 1972. Tower House was demolished in 1988 and replaced with Priory Gardens from June 2001.

To date no records have been found that detail who purchased the different lots offered in the sale of October 1846 and it has not been possible to identify a builder for Thorpe House. Regrettably despite an extensive search it appears that original documents relating to ownership prior to 1998 are no longer available.

There is no mention of Portswood (32 Priory Road); Thorpe House (34), St. Ronan's (36) or Chalford (38) in the 1841 and 1851 censuses, and they do not appear on the map for 1852 suggesting that they were all built after that date.

Plan Ref. mp 29 held by the Malvern Hills Conservators, (Fig. 3) records the positions of houses that were already standing by October 1854 when the plan was drawn. It does not give any indication of when they were built but it clearly shows Thorpe House; the footprint of the house depicted matches that seen on plans of St. Clare. It also shows that Portswood and Chalford were already built; St. Ronan's was built later.

Original documents for St. Ronan's, now in the possession of the current owners, John and Carol Hutber, show that the property was built by George McCann for Joseph Wilton in 1856. The plans show the owner of the adjacent plot to the north (no. 34) as Rev. J. W. A. Taylor. Rev. Taylor is known to have run a preparatory school at Portswood between 1853 and 1858; he then sold Portswood and opened Rookery School in Headington, Oxford which was intended as a preparatory school for Eton and Harrow.

Portswood was built in 1853; a plaque above the rear doorway shows this date inscribed below the monogram JWAT, now known to stand for John William Augustus Taylor. It is likely that the property at 34 Priory Road, Malvern, Worcestershire, was built at about the same time. If Rev. Taylor was responsible for building Thorpe House then he did not attempt to match the construction of Portswood suggesting that it was a speculative build.

Eye witness accounts of the building have been difficult to find and knowledge of its appearance came originally from a photograph taken by Roger Hall Jones immediately prior to its demolition in November 1988.

Fig. 9 is a photograph, kindly provided by Anne Noble, of the property circa 1950 showing the main front entrance door.

Fig. 9   The Clans Private Hotel, Circa 1950

The building consisted of a cellar, three floors and an attic and the following plan of the ground floor (Fig. 10) is based on that for Tower House drawn in 1982.

Fig. 10 Plan of the Ground Floor of the Building

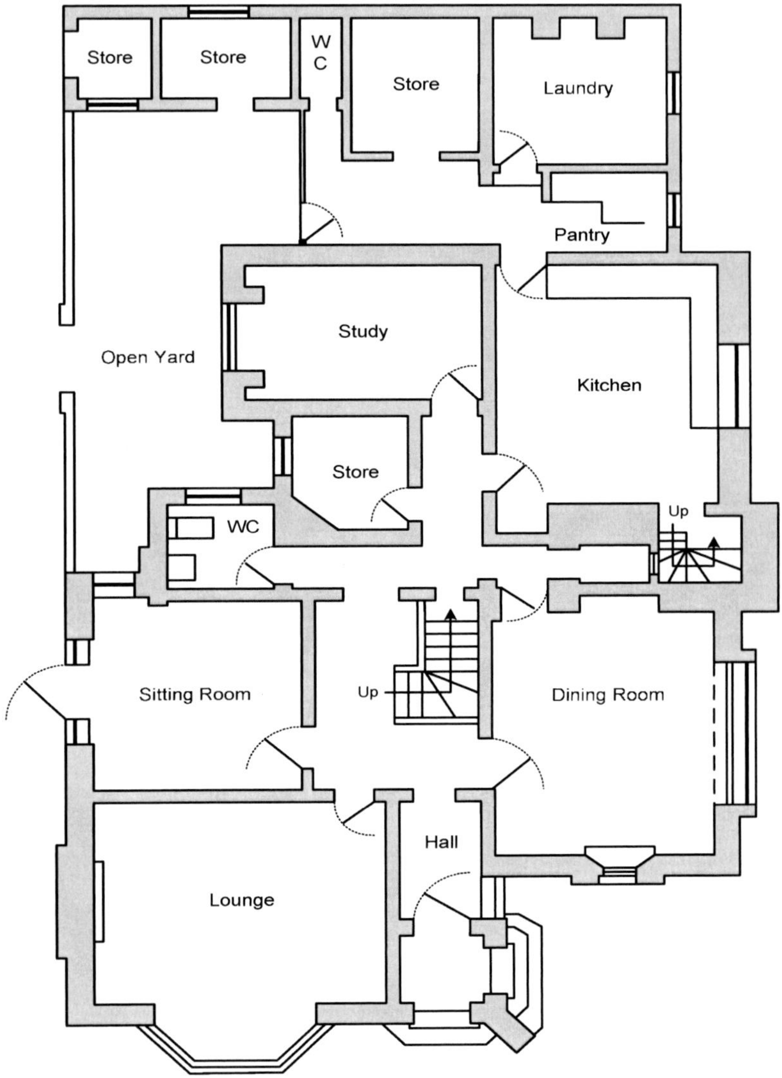

A plan of the site of Tower House in 1982 is shown in Fig. 11. The greenhouse was not standing in 1982 but it is shown where it was located in earlier plans. A suggestion that this was not a good site for a greenhouse, receiving sunlight for only part of the day is based on the situation of the present property but when it was built some 150 years ago it would have been acceptable. It was on the south side of the building aligned East – West which would allow maximum use of available light, particularly in the Winter and Spring. The original house was further from the boundary wall with St. Ronan's and there would not have been the amount of tree cover there is at present.

Anne Noble reports that there was no green house when her grandparents bought the house in 1950 but only a 'large well-built shed with deep windows on one side giving good light'; presumably this was the 'Lumber Shed' depicted on the plan.

The path from the pedestrian entrance had been redirected at some time so that it went to the rear of the building rather than parallel with the road as shown in 1886. Anne said that it still went parallel to the road in the 1950s so it must have been altered after 1962 when her grandparents sold the property.

Fig. 11 Plan of the site in 1982

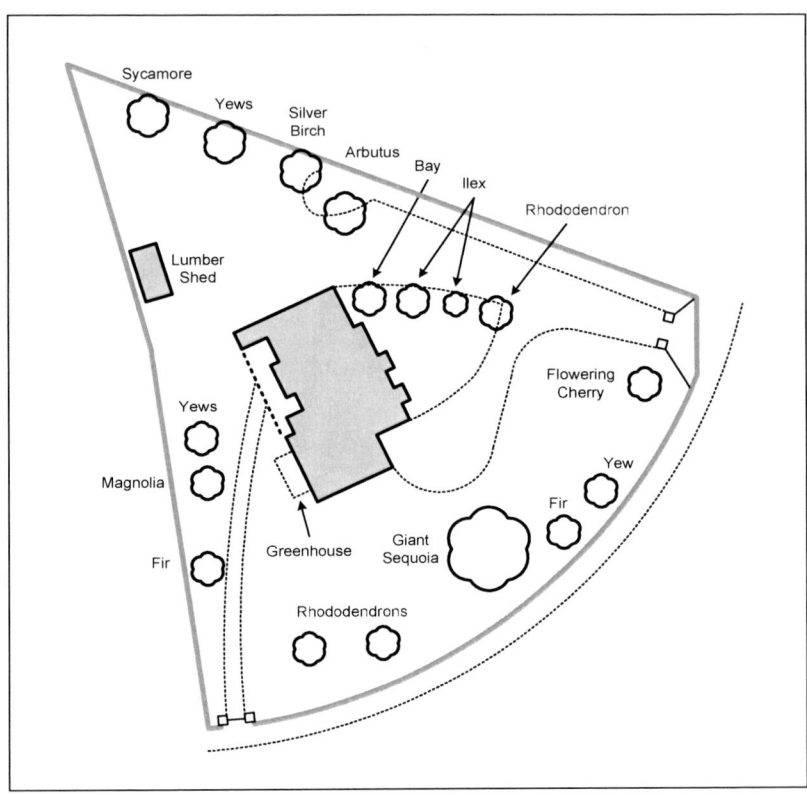

The Victorian influence on the site is strong with the buildings to either side of the plot, Portswood and St Ronan's being notably flamboyant, with gothic influence and many local design features such as varied roof-scapes, turrets, strong chimney stacks, eaves and verge detailing and varied and individual fenestrations. Nikolaus Pevsner, in his book 'Worcestershire – Architectural Guides. Buildings of England', describes these buildings as 'Jacobean' and uses the term 'crow-stepped' to describe the broken style of the eaves of Portswood.

The south east elevation of Thorpe House has a front gable with a hierarchy of window size including a large ground floor bay window. The elevation also includes a hexagonal corner turret. The building was constructed in brick with features of stone such as the surrounds to metal window frames. St. Ronan's, situated at one side of Thorpe House, was of similar construction. On the other side, Portswood is an example of the more expensive construction using dressed Malvern stone, again with stone window surrounds and metal window frames.

Winstanley, which originally stood opposite Thorpe House, and Chalford, were also constructed of stone and were typical of many, but by no means all of the houses in the area

Since it was considerably easier, quicker and cheaper to build using regular bricks rather than the hard, difficult to work, more expensive stone, it is possible that Thorpe House was erected by a speculative builder hoping to cash-in on the expansion by renting it out to visitors to Malvern. This could also explain the rather less decorated exterior when compared to neighbouring properties. No evidence has been found that the builder actually lived in the house at any time.

A photograph taken by John Noble in 1950 of 34 Priory Road from the roadside (Fig. 12) shows what was supposed to be a family crest set between the upper windows. Anne Noble reported that her grandparents had been told that the original house had been built for the Lord Lieutenant of the County and that this was his crest, although it was accepted that this might have been 'a myth'.

No evidence for this has been found. The Lord Lieutenant from 1839 to 1876 was George William Lyttleton, 4th Baron Lyttleton, Baron of Frankley. He was not a direct descendant of Apphia, Lady Lyttleton, 2nd wife of Thomas Lyttleton, 2nd Baron of Frankley, who founded the Lyttleton (or Littleton) School at the Priory, because she and her husband died childless and the baronetcy died out. It was later recreated and it was to this branch that George William belonged. He committed suicide by throwing himself down the stairs at Hagley Hall, the family seat.

Further research has shown that the symbol, which shows a single snake climbing a staff, is a representation of the Staff of Asclepius and not a family crest; this is the correct symbol for the medical profession rather than the Caduceus which shows two inter-twined snakes around a staff. It is believed that it could have been added to the building sometime after it was built.

Fig. 12 Front View Of The Clans Hotel

Comparison of John's photograph with that taken by Roger Hall Jones in 1988 appears to show that there may have been some alterations made to this symbol at some time.

Anne Noble (nee Burcher) remembers the house when her grandparents ran it as The Clans Hotel from 1950 to 1964. All her family holidays were spent at the hotel and she has fond memories of the time spent there.

She described the entrance hall with its marble floor, adding that there was always a large flower arrangement there, provided by her grandmother Esme Noble. Outside the front door there was a sequoia set in a lawn. This is discussed in more detail later.

In addition to the main staircase there was a smaller, spiral staircase that led from the hall to the original servant's room which was used by her grandfather, William Noble. This is presumed to be the single room in the tower referred to by Joyce Sutcliffe.

Anne remembers the heavy Victorian furniture in the reception rooms and private sitting room and commented on the marble fireplace beneath the window set within the chimney breast. At Christmas time Esme always displayed a nativity scene there (Fig. 13).

Winstanley, on the opposite side of Priory Road, can be seen through the window.

Fig. 13 Fireplace beneath Lounge Window.

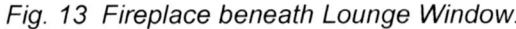

The lounge faced the road and the dining room overlooked what is now the car park.

Beyond the reception rooms there was a large kitchen with a heavy pine table that was kept well-scrubbed. There were storerooms and also a dairy which at the time still contained a butter churn that had been used by earlier occupants. Outside there was an open courtyard that led to a lawn where, in addition to many smaller shrubs, there was a large magnolia tree, sadly now removed, and a second sequoia. This caused some of the rooms to be very shaded but could not be removed as it had a preservation order on it.

The gate at the pedestrian entrance was hung on the opposite pillar to that which is now used and the path turned sharply to the right running parallel to the road between the wall and the holly tree, still there today, before turning towards the front door. She suggested that the original building came about as far as the end of the central bay at the front of Priory Gardens so that it was further from St. Ronan's than the current building.

Norman Brown of Malvern U3A Family History Group has also provided personal memories of The Clans Hotel. He describes it as 'a most impressive building with a large tiled entrance hall, an imposing central staircase splitting into two at the first landing getting narrower and steeper at each level'.

His future wife was living in a bedsit at the hotel at the time and he says that there seemed to be 'a lot of permanent residents, mostly old ladies'. He pointed out that the presence of the old ladies 'combined with the tiled hall, which seemed to magnify the sound of footsteps, made it quite difficult to visit undiscovered'; needless to say he didn't elaborate on this!

He also recalls arriving back at The Clans after their first date 'in the early hours of Sunday morning' and finding the Hotel locked and all the windows secured so that it was impossible to get in. His mother's response, on finding the young lady at their home the following morning is not recorded! 18 months later they were married. He commented that The Clans seemed more like a residential home than a hotel.

Joyce Sutcliffe (formerly Howard), who ran the building as Hotel St. Clare from 1969 to 1972, described it as 'a really beautiful, elegant building' which she was sad to leave. She was also able to give a description of the interior of the building which she had been told owed much to the ideas brought back by the 'original owner', or more likely Edward Ratheram, from the 'European Tour' and incorporated into the building.

From the gardens, which included lawns, flower beds and a vegetable garden, the main entrance, sheltered by a porch, was via steps into an elegant hall which led to the lounge facing the road, with the dining room on the side facing towards Portswood. Towards the rear of the building was the kitchen and utility area leading to an enclosed court yard.

The plaster ceilings were elaborately decorated and there was a half landing on the main staircase which had an impressive stained glass window. Joyce confirmed the fireplaces set beneath the window and she recalls the chimneys could be swept from the outside of the building removing the need for a chimney sweep to enter the rooms.

At the time, Joyce says that there were 9 bedrooms, 7 doubles and 2 singles, one off the main stair case and set above the main entrance, the other in the tower at the side of the building and reached by its own staircase.

There were gas fires in the bedrooms and, unusually, there were no locks on any internal doors except for the toilet, which Joyce described as 'a very elegant, wood panelled room' fitted with an unusual 'three seated lavatory'. It was not, however, intended for multi occupation since only the central area was fitted with a highly decorated toilet pan.

A Sequoia Dendron Gigantean (Giant Sequoia, Giant California Redwood), incorrectly named a Wellingtonia, is located at the front of the site and is a protected species. It was first brought into cultivation by a Scotsman, John D. Mathew, who collected seeds from the Calaveras Grove, in California, USA, and brought them to Scotland in August 1853.

A further seed collection from the same location made by William Lobb from Cornwall, acting for the Veitch Nursery (1808 to 1969), at Budlake near Exeter, arrived in England in December 1853. Seed from this batch was widely distributed throughout Europe and is probably the source of the tree on the site.

The Giant Sequoia is the world's largest tree and grows to 330 feet high. The oldest example is 3,500 years old. Trees planted in Britain in 1854 are now typically 150 feet tall, the tallest being at Benmore, Scotland, which is 180 feet tall.

The girth of the Priory Gardens tree was first measured as 17 feet on the 28th April 2011, at a height of 5 feet from the ground on the north side of the tree. By April 2012 the girth measured 17.14 feet; this rate of increase suggests the tree was planted early in the life of Thorpe House; it could not, in any case, have been planted before January 1854.

Further measurements taken in November 2012 show growth rate to have been abnormally high due to the record level of rainfall; they are, therefore, of no value in estimating the age of the tree.

The fir tree located to the west of the site had a girth of 11 feet 5 and 11/16th inches when measured at a height of 4.5 feet from the ground on the 28th October 2011

The Yew tree to the west of the building was cut down in 2009 following complaints of restriction of sunlight by a leaseholder of Priory Gardens.

The tree was 76 years old and hence planted in about 1933, presumably by Dr John Phelps. Yew trees can live up to 3000 years and two thirds of the yew trees currently alive in Britain were extant in biblical times.

Entries in the Malvern Advertiser from its first edition on the 16th of June 1855 show the occupants of Thorpe House as 'Visitors' and consideration of these entries suggest that it may have been a multi-occupied building at that time. In addition to Edward and Harriet Ratheram other 'visitors' included Mrs Ames and family, Mrs Finch, Miss Wilde-Brown and Hon. Mrs H. Noel.

It is unlikely that it was a Lodging House since there does not appear to be a regular resident who could be considered to be a 'Lodging House Keeper'; also Thorpe House does not appear in the Commercial section of Billings Directory of 1855 where other lodging Houses in the area are recorded.

The change from 'Visitor' to 'Resident' in the Malvern Gazette entry dated the 18th of August 1855 is believed to indicate the date of the sale of the property to Edward Ratheram.

2. Family Histories of Main Owners or Occupiers c.1855 – 1985

2.1 Edward Ratheram (Thorpe House c.1855 to 1871)

Edward Ratheram was born at Kings Norton about 1826 as recorded in census records, but no baptism record has been found. He was the second child of Charles Ratheram, who was born in Birmingham in about 1790, according to census and other records seen, and Harriet Ratheram (poss. nee Porter) who was born about 1800 (possibly in Islington, London).

A record of a baptism on 17th of August 1787 has been found for Charles, son of Charles and Elizabeth Ratheram of Nether Whitacre, Warwickshire, on the Warwickshire Baptisms, Marriage and Burials records for 1538-1812 (Ancestry). Since these records also include baptisms for other children of this couple, giving names which agree with those of known sisters of Charles Ratheram, it is believed that this could be the correct family.

A marriage record referring to the marriage by licence of Charles Ratheram of Birmingham (the parish was illegible) and Harriot Porter (sic) of Southwark at Christchurch, Southwark on the 2nd of October 1822 has been found in 'London, England, Marriages and Banns, 1754-1821; Samuel Porter is given as a witness. This would appear to agree with a possible baptism record for Harriot, daughter of Samuel Porter and Elizabeth in Islington on the 20th of January 1799 recorded in 'London, England, Baptisms, Marriages and Burials, 1538-1812'.

Pigot's Directory (Reference to Birmingham) for 1828 gives Charles' occupation as 'Plater' and in the census taken on the 6th of June 1841 the family is recorded as living at The Henburys, Moseley, Kings Norton, Worcestershire, a large mansion house set in 40 acres of parkland; all birthplaces are given as 'Not Worcestershire'.

They employed one male servant and two female servants at the time. This is the only census record for Charles and his wife as they both died soon afterwards – Harriet in 1843 and Charles, who died of liver disease, on the 17th July 1845 in Kings Heath, Kings Norton; it is most likely that they both died at The Henburys even though the address appears to be slightly different. The Death Duty Register for 1845 shows that Edward paid death duty at Birmingham on Charles' estate.

It is possible that the Ratheram family had been involved in the silver and plating industry since the 1780s; references to a Charles Ratheram, silver plate manufacturer, Great Charles Street, Birmingham, have been found in trade directories from this time – it is likely that this was the grandfather of Edward Ratheram. The London Gazette for the 5th of January 1813 records the dissolution of a partnership between Charles Ratheram and Thomas Wharton, (later to marry Elizabeth Ratheram, sister of Charles), Jewellers and gilt toy makers, which could well refer to this older Charles. Both are later listed separately in Great Charles Street, Birmingham.

The London Gazette for the 1st of October 1825 records a similar occurrence between Joseph Creed and Charles Ratheram (believed to be the father of Edward) and both of these gentlemen are separately listed as silver platers in Pigot's Directory for 1837; Joseph Creed in Carver Street, Birmingham and Charles Ratheram at 133 Great Charles Street, Birmingham and 29 Bartlett's Buildings, near Fetter Lane, London. This latter address is confirmed in the records for Sun Fire Office from December 1826 – March 1832 where Charles is recorded as 'Silver plater and hardwareman'.

Charles Ratheram is also recorded as a manufacturer of Sheffield plate in both Birmingham and London up to 1845, the year of his death, in 'Sheffield Plate- its history ...' by H. N. Veitch. No record has been found for a hallmark or makers mark referring to Charles Ratheram, and the Birmingham Assay Office and Sheffield Assay

Office have confirmed that they have no records for this name; the Jewellery Quarter Museum was also unable to help.

Wider investment activities and interests have been found for Charles Ratheram, including an attempt to set up a soap manufacturing business; involvement in the proposed 'Grand Connection' railway line between Wolverhampton and Worcester; involvement with the development of the Birmingham to Gloucester Railway line and the proposed 'Birmingham and Derby Junction Railway' which aimed to unite the 'North Midland', 'London and Birmingham', 'Grand Junction' and 'Birmingham and Gloucester' Railway companies.

He served on the provisional committees of several of these ventures, as reported in both the Birmingham Gazette and Bristol Mercury at various times in the 1830's and 1840's. His business associates included Thomas Lane of Moundsley Hall, Kings Norton and John and William Dent who bought Sudeley Castle in 1837, sons of the founder of Dent's, Glove Makers of Worcester; a firm still in production today, although the factory is now in Warminster, Wiltshire.

One of his last meetings, reported in Berrow's Worcester Journal for the 6th of March 1845, would have been that which confirmed the 'lease in perpetuity' of the 'Birmingham and Gloucester Railway' to 'Midland Railways'. In 1840 Charles had sold a parcel of land from The Henburys estate to the 'Birmingham and Gloucester Railway Company' enabling the line to be built, effectively cutting off the farm, which formed part of the extensive estate, from the rest of the grounds.

Newspaper reports from the Birmingham Gazette of 1832 and 1836 suggest an interest in local politics, where he is recorded as a signatory to various letters to the retiring MP and complaints regarding the activities of the 'Political Union'.

He also had a keen interest in horticulture, being listed in records for the Birmingham Botanical and Horticultural Society for several years. One example from the Birmingham Gazette for May 1835 records that he won prizes for the best dish of grapes, best fruiting lemon tree and best dish of forced potatoes. The same year he received 'Special Awards' for 3 broccoli heads; spinach and lettuce; grapes, and a tropical plant. Whether he actually worked in the garden himself or employed gardeners to do the work for him is not known.

This interest is reflected in the provision of a vinery, hot house and green houses at The Henburys as recorded in the description of the estate in the Birmingham Gazette for the 8th of December 1845, when it was put up for lease following his death.

A copy of the Will of Charles Ratheram, signed on the 31st of May 1845, obtained from National Archives is very difficult to read, being illegible in places but, under the terms of the Will, Edward inherited the business while Harriet received a bequest of money; it was not possible to read the actual sum involved.

The Will is complicated but it is understood that the freehold estate, consisting of The Henburys house and grounds, though not the contents of the house, was left in trust, to be managed as they saw fit by the Trustees, Edward Ratheram, Benjamin Pearson Bartleet and Jesse Bartleet (both Solicitors). Any profit from income and rent was to be for the sole use of Harriet, not 'any husband or husbands she might take', or after her death any children that she might have, until such time that they reached 'their majority', when the estate could be sold by the trustees and the proceeds shared equally among any issue, male or female. Only if Harriet died without lawful issue did the freehold estate go to Edward.

Leasehold properties, railway and company shares, securities and ready money, household furnishings and effects, and all the rest of his estate, were however left to Edward. Provision was made for the replacement of any trustees who were unable to continue in that position and Edward and Benjamin and Jesse Bartleet were named as Executors before the Will was signed. Several additions and alterations were signed by Charles on the 3rd of June 1845.

There was, however, a codicil attached which appears to revoke part of the provision made for Edward. All the household furniture and implements, which were listed in detail, including glassware, silverware, wines, pictures, books and 'all other moveable effects not being fixtures within the dwelling in my occupation' (namely The Henburys), and also 'horses, carriages, hot house and greenhouse plants', were left to Harriet.

He also made two bequests, free of duty, to his sisters; £30 (£3,000 at 2012) to Elizabeth Wharton wife of Thomas Wharton, another plater, and £19 9s (£1,945 at 2012 values) to Frances Earl, widow of John Earl. With these exceptions the original Will was ratified, and Charles signed the codicil in the presence of witnesses Elizabeth Wharton and Tertius I Cook, clerk to Mr Bartleet, solicitor on the 15th of July 1845. He died two days later.

The Birmingham Gazette for the 8th of December 1845 published a notice offering The Henburys for lease giving a full description of the property, applications to view to be made to Edward Ratheram at Great Charles Street or Bartleet, Solicitors.

Birmingham Assay Office records show that Edward registered the maker's mark 'EM' in 1847, giving the address of 133 Great Charles Street, and the 1849 Post Office Directory for Birmingham and 'History and Directory, Alphabetical List, for Birmingham' both give Edward as 'Manufacturer of Silver and Plated Wares', 133 Great Charles Street, Birmingham, with his home address as Monument House, Monument Lane, Edgbaston, Birmingham.

In the census taken on the 6th of June 1841, 133 Great Charles Street was recorded as occupied by George Wilkinson and family, some of whom were involved in small metal work – bit making and die sinking being recorded; there was no apparent reference to plating at this time.

Before 1840 plating was achieved by pressing two plates of metal together and applying heat. Electroplating was developed for commercial use in the Jewellery Quarter of Birmingham and patented by George R. Elkington in 1840. Its success was rapid despite requiring a local source of electricity.

The first dynamo was made in 1832 and 'The Canning Story 1785-1985' – the history of the firm William Canning Ltd of Birmingham - records that Daniell Cells or Smee Batteries were used for plating up to the 1870's. The first dynamo specifically designed for use in the plating industry was patented by J. S. Woolrich in 1842. Thomas Prime built a dynamo to the design of Woolrich the same year which he used at his Birmingham Works. This machine was seen in operation by Michael Faraday in 1845 and can now be seen in the Birmingham City Museum Department of Science and Industry.

It was to be about 30 years before the dynamo replaced batteries on a regular basis. Although high pressure steam engines were built by Richard Trevithick from 1800 onwards centrally located electricity generating stations did not start until 1881.

Anyone taking up electroplating before 1860 would have required a license from George Elkington, however, it is likely that Edward was sufficiently motivated to take up the new technology sometime between 1851 and 1861. The 1851 census dated the 30th of March records John Kilner at 133 Great Charles Street as 'silver plate worker', but by the 7th of April 1861 he is described as 'journeyman silver and electroplate worker'.

Potassium and silver cyanide, were both used in the plating process, and are deadly poisons. It is likely that William Canning Ltd were the suppliers of plating chemicals to Messrs Ratheram, being one of the major suppliers at the time.

Whilst not being a cumulative poison, regular low level exposure to cyanides can cause a number of debilitating symptoms; even handling contaminated clothing would be sufficient to cause problems. Awareness of the danger seems to have been minimal and the Jewellery Museum in the Jewellery Quarter shows cyanide being stored in the same cupboard as tea and sugar. Cyanide salts and granulated sugar are virtually identical in appearance.

On the 19th of August 1850 The Birmingham Gazette published an advert offering Monument House and its adjoining 'family residence in the occupation of Mr Ratheram' for lease. Similar adverts appeared for several weeks.

On the 27th of January 1851 the same paper announced the sale by auction on the 3rd of February of 'very desirable residences in Edgbaston'. The announcement included a full description of Monument House and its gardens and out buildings and the adjoining residence, its gardens and outbuildings, and included 'the lofty, picturesque building known as 'The Monument' (also known as 'Perrott's Folly')' and a plantation fronting on to Water Works Road. The house occupied by Mr Ratheram was said to be available from Michaelmas 1851; Monument House was unoccupied.

The sale was apparently unsuccessful because on the 30th of March 1851, Edward and his sister Harriet are recorded at Monument Lane with one male servant and one female servant; Edward's occupation is given as 'Manufacturer'. In the same census 133 Great Charles Street is recorded as occupied by John Kilner, as previously mentioned.

There followed further adverts in The Birmingham Gazette in both March and September 1851 now offering the property for rent from Michaelmas.

The first reference to the Ratherams in the Malvern area was found in the Worcester Chronicle and Provincial Railway Gazette for the 17th of September 1851 when 'Mr Ratheram and friends' are recorded 'among the throng' attending the 2nd Malvern Flower Show in 'the field south of Graham Road'. Further evidence of their presence in the town has also been found.

Berrow's Worcester Journal of the 29th of July 1852 lists Edward Ratheram and Miss Ratheram amongst the 'Arrivals' in Malvern, but it gives no indication of where they might be living at the time, although it is likely that the house in Monument Lane had been given up and there is the probability that they were renting a property in Malvern from about that date.

The Birmingham Gazette for the 28th of March 1853 announced a sale by auction, to be held on the 12th and 13th of April, at Monument House, Monument Lane, of household items including all manner of furniture and fittings, decorative items, curtains, beds and baths, 28 dozen bottles of port and sherry, the contents of the kitchen and pantry and outdoor items such as a 'Baddings Patent Mowing Machine'.

The sale was at the direction of Edward Ratheram 'who was changing his residence'. It does not say whether the contents came from Monument House itself or from the 'family residence' described earlier. However, it seems reasonable to assume the house previously occupied by Edward and Harriet was also sold by this time. Later that same year Monument House was again offered for lease eventually being used as a school.

Edward Ratheram was certainly resident in Malvern when, on the 22nd of February 1854, the Worcester Chronicle and Provincial Railway Gazette carried a report that one Thomas Garnes was charged with embezzling from 'his master' 'Edward Ratheram of Malvern', £20 5s (£2,250 at 2012 values) with which he had been entrusted to pay bills. He had been arrested at a Cheltenham address on the 15th of February after jumping out of an upstairs window and being apprehended by a waiting constable. He claimed to have thrown a purse containing a watch and ten sovereigns out of the window but nothing was found. He was brought before the bench again the following day and committed for trial.

A further report in the Worcester Chronicle records that on the 1st of March 1854, Thomas Garnes age 19, Footman to Edward Ratheram, was charged that on the 8th of February 1854 he stole £20 5s, the property of Mr Ratheram; he was found guilty of the crime and given 1 years imprisonment.

Census records show that the home address for Thomas Garnes was 1 Long Passage, Cheltenham and that was probably where he was arrested. It seems that he did not learn from his experience – the England and Wales Criminal Register records that in 1856 at Gloucester Trinity Quarter Sessions he was convicted of larceny of £5 (£440 at 2012 values) from a dwelling house and, due to his previous conviction, was sentenced to 4 years penal servitude, the original punishment of 'transportation' being crossed out on the record.

The large sum of money entrusted to Thomas Garnes suggests that Edward was making considerable purchases late 1853 to early 1854; it is possible that he was in the process of furnishing a new residence in Malvern.

Several entries in Berrow's Worcester Gazette during August and September 1855 list Mr E. Rotheram (sic) and Miss Rotheram (sic) as 'visitors' to Malvern and the 1st edition of The Malvern Advertiser, dated the 16th of June 1855, records Mr E. Ratheram and Miss Ratheram as visitors at Thorpe House; similar entries appear until the 4th of August 1855.

During this time other residents are occasionally recorded at Thorpe House in addition to the Ratherams; thus it seems that Thorpe House was a multi occupied property.

From the edition of the Malvern Advertiser dated the 18th of August 1855, until the paper ceased publication for 8 months in October 1855, Edward and Harriet are listed as the sole 'Residents' of Thorpe House. This suggests it is possible that Edward became the owner of Thorpe House in August 1855.

The 1855 Billings directory for Worcestershire records Edward Rotheram (sic) resident at Thorpe House, Malvern but this is believed to be an alternative spelling, which also occurred in newspaper entries and the census of 1861.

When the Malvern Advertiser was again published on the 5th of July 1856 Edward and Harriet are recorded as residents at Sutherland House, Malvern, which was listed in the 1860 P.O. Directory as a Lodging House. They moved to The Cedars, another Lodging House, for three weeks in August/September 1856 and then returned to Sutherland House until the beginning of October. Throughout this time Thorpe House, or St. Clare as it became known from the 19th of July 1856, was apparently empty.

As no records have been found as to what was occurring at Thorpe House/St. Clare, it is suggested that, after buying the property, Edward decided to make alterations, possibly improving the interior so that it appeared more as described earlier. There would also have been building work proceeding next door because St. Ronan's was first recorded as occupied on the 11th of October 1856.

Edward and Harriet were briefly described as resident at St. Clare on that date, but from January 1857 onwards they are consistently recorded there. There can be little doubt that Edward Ratheram was a house owner in Malvern by 1857 since the Worcester Chronicle dated the 4th of March 1857 records that he was a signatory on the Ratepayers Memorial at a meeting of Malvern Commissioners. He was unlikely to be classed as a ratepayer if he was only renting a property.

The 1857 Malvern Horticultural show was also the first at which Edward is recorded as a prize winner, as his father had been at the Birmingham Horticultural Show some 20 years earlier. A report carried by the Hereford Times for the 11th of July 1857 about the annual show in Malvern, described as 'this gay and fashionable town', lists him as gaining first prizes for 'Balsams' and 'best device of cut flowers'.

It would seem that he must have had an established garden by this time to enable him to reach such a high standard. St. Clare was known to have had a greenhouse and a fairly extensive garden. Miss Ratheram was included in the 'large and fashionable gathering of 1857'. From this show onwards Edward is recorded as a prize winner each year until at least 1865.

Although there is no indication given of their address, both Edward and Harriet are listed in the Worcester Chronicle for the 4th of July 1860 as making subscriptions of £5 5s each (£525 at 2012 values) to Malvern Priory Church Restoration Fund.

The census taken on the 7th of April 1861 shows that Edward and Harriet are living at St. Clare, Priory Road, Great Malvern with two servants. No occupation is recorded for Edward at this time; John Kilner is still living and working at 133 Great Charles Street.

A report in Birmingham Daily Post of the 28th of January 1864 tells of the attempted suicide of John Kilmer (sic) age 73, a silversmith, at 133 Great Charles Street. He was said to have worked as foreman for Messrs Ratheram for 40 years, living at the house for 20 years. The firm had operated from 'extensive shopping at the rear of the building' until Messrs Ratheram retired from trade in 1863, being replaced by a Mr Redfern.

Kilmer had lost his job, although he was led to believe by 'his masters' that he could remain at the house. Mr Redfern wanted the house for himself and although he was preparing the house next door for Kilmer, the old man, who had recently lost his wife, was sufficiently upset by the circumstances in which he found himself, after long service with the same firm, to make an attempt on his own life.

Edward, at this time, was apparently spending his retirement from trade, gardening in Malvern, being awarded second prize for gooseberries in 1863 and second prize for fuchsias in 1865 as reported in the Birmingham Daily Post giving the results for Malvern Horticultural Shows of those years.

His interest in gardening probably began at The Henburys, a former home, since it is recorded by 'The Friends of Highbury Park' as having extensive gardens and greenhouses, housing fairly exotic plants. A later owner, G. F. Lyndon presented a double white Camellia to Birmingham Botanical Gardens in 1893 which was thought to have been growing in the greenhouses at The Henburys since the early 19th century, which means that it would have been growing there during the Ratheram residency.

The Worcestershire Chronicle for the 30th of January 1867 includes a report of 4th Annual Meeting of Shareholders of the Malvern Proprietary College Company at which Edward Ratheram, presumably as a shareholder, is recorded as seconding the appointment of treasurer and auditors for the coming year. His interest in the College was likely to have been purely a business interest since neither he nor Harriet had any children of their own but Edward would undoubtedly have been aware that the nephew of his two close associates, Thomas Lane and William Makin, was amongst the early pupils at the College.

These gentlemen were both married to daughters of Charles Shaw, a wealthy industrialist from Birmingham, and a younger daughter, Caroline Julia Shaw, married John Devereux Muntz, a partner in Sims and Muntz, Iron Founders, Aston Junction Forge in Birmingham. Their eldest son, Devereux Shaw Muntz, was a boarder at the College from September 1866 to the end of the Midsummer term in 1869; it is possible that this is the source of Edward's interest in the College.

Unfortunately a search made by the College Archivist found no further reference to Edward's activities there.

On the 29th of January 1871 Edward died at Wrington in Somerset, his age was recorded as 45. His death was notified by the Coroner for Somerset at Shepton Mallet. The cause of death was stated as 'overdose of chloral hydrate taken through ignorance of its strength'.
A report of the Coroner's Inquest in the Bristol Mercury for the 4th of February 1871 records that, at the time of his death, Edward had been living with a Dr. Barnes at Wrington since July 1870, leaving his terminally ill sister in the care of servants, in an attempt to rid himself of an addiction to opium; he had been a user for 25 years, the whole of his adult life. From census records for 1871, Dr. Barnes is believed to be Dr. George Barnes, of School House, Wrington, registered address in the Medical Register for 1871 being given as Newcastle, Staffs.

It is reported that on Thursday the 26th of January 1871 Edward had used Dr. Barnes' name to obtain an 8oz bottle of chloral hydrate, a sedative that had only been registered in 1869, from the chemist Ferris and Company, 4&5 Union Street, Bristol; this is strongly denied by the chemist who claimed they would not have supplied such a quantity of chloral hydrate, but that he was actually given 8oz. of chloral syrup, containing 10 grains of chloral hydrate per teaspoon, somewhat less potent than chloral hydrate. This would, however, still be poisonous, but only if taken in very large quantities; it is not a controlled substance in the UK.

Edward was found on the floor of his room by Dr. Barnes on the morning of the 29th of January 1871; Dr. Barnes immediately sent for a colleague, Mr Chadwick. Although Edward was alive at the time Mr Chadwick arrived, he died soon afterwards. The two doctors then conducted their own post mortem examination, finding nothing physically wrong and concluding that the death was due to an overdose.

Whilst this report answers many questions about Edward's demise it raises doubts in respect of the standard of treatment and supervision provided by Dr. Barnes.

Edward's actions are believed to be typical of the behaviour of a drug addict and he had consumed a considerable quantity of the syrup; the result of many years of opium abuse could have resulted in the effects of choral hydrate being exaggerated, causing unexpected death. Since tolerance for chloral hydrate is readily acquired it is likely that he had not taken this substance before.

How and why he began taking opium, not an unusual occurrence for the time, is not known, but it is most likely the actions of a well-to-do young man with money and time to spare, who wished to experience some of the more vicarious activities of the Victorian era. Edward began using the substance in about 1845, when he was still under the age of 20, and possibly at the time of his father's death when he took over the family firm. If Edward had undertaken the 'European tour' as suggested by Joyce Sutcliffe it was likely that he was taking opium during the time he was on this journey.

Edward was buried on the 4th of February 1871 in Malvern Cemetery, Madresfield Road, Malvern, reference Grave number 1797 Plot 4. This is situated close to the Sextons Office, now the Lodge, one of the most expensive parts of the cemetery at the time. The cost of the burial was £5 5s (£515 at 2012 values). The grave is marked by a head stone and elaborate tomb which the current cemetery manager estimates would cost about £8,000 in 2012. The inscription reads "In loving remembrance of Edward Ratheram late of St. Clare, Great Malvern who died Jan 29 1871 aged 45 years". It makes no reference to the place of death.

Edward's Will was written in 1867 (he would have been aged about 40) and he left the entirety of his estate, shown by the grant of probate of the 3rd of March 1871 to be around £6,000 (£588,000 at 2012 values), to Harriet, but only for her lifetime. Under the terms of the Will the house and contents then passed to Thomas Lane; the remainder of the estate passed to his executors Thomas Lane of Moundsley Hall, Kings Norton; William Makin of St. Clare, Sandfield Park, Liverpool and William Corner West, Physician, of Great Malvern, for disposal according to the detailed instructions he gave concerning his remaining assets, and for the setting up of a trust for the benefit of Helen Elizabeth Makin wife of William Makin, or any of her surviving children who attained the age of 21.

The reason for this decision or the relationship with this lady is not known. She was born Helen Elizabeth Shaw on the 29th of March 1822 in Birmingham, and she lived at Greenfield House, Harbourne Road, Edgbaston, very close to Monument Lane where Edward and Harriet had lived, until her marriage to widower William Makin in 1851; perhaps they were friends from that time.

A codicil to the will gave a legacy, free of duty, of £100 (£9,800 at 2012 values) to William Corner West M.D.; the Death Duty Register for 1871 shows that Thomas Lane paid death duty on Edward's estate at Worcester although the sum involved is not given.

A report in the Birmingham Daily Post for June 1871 regarding a future sale by his Executors, shows that Edward still had an interest in the house and land at The Henburys, Moseley, a substantial property which was occupied by a tenant, Walter Lyndon, Managing Director of Minerva Works, Fazeley Street, Birmingham, manufacturer of edge tools; there was still 3 years left on the lease.

Walter Lyndon bought the property which, on his death in 1875, passed to his son George Frederick Lyndon, described as 'one of the foremost public men of the Moseley and Kings Heath District'; a magistrate, county councillor, keen sportsman and gardener.

In 1890 Richard Cadbury purchased a plot of agricultural land on The Henburys estate to build Uffculme House and in 1893 bought the rest of the estate, which then passed to his son Barrow Cadbury, who sold it to Birmingham Civic Society in 1923 for £9,000 (£423,000 at 2012 values). Together with the grounds of Uffculme House and Highbury House, former home of Joseph Chamberlain, it now forms Highbury Park.

All that remains of The Henburys today, apart from the kitchen garden wall, is an obelisk built in an area known from before 1840 as 'Monument Field', first thought to have been built by Walter Lyndon but attributed by G. F. Lyndon to 'a former owner, a Mr Ratheram'; it's age would suggest that this was Charles rather than Edward. These details come from a record by 'The Friends of Highbury Park'.

A notice posted by Solicitors J. Bartleet in the London Gazette for the 9th of May 1871, requesting contact from anyone with a claim against the estate, links Edward with Bartlett's Buildings in London, which suggests that he still owned an interest in that premises in addition to St. Clare and The Henburys.

Helen Elizabeth Makin died at St. Clare, Sandfield Park, Liverpool on the 1st of January 1873; William was granted limited administration of her estate of under £450, (£41,850 at 2012 values) revised to under £800 (£74,400 at 2012 values) in May 1874. She left four children eligible to benefit from Edward's Trust if they survived to 21 years of age and records show that they all did so.

Two of her sons became respected breeders of Hereford cattle and well known as church leaders in Lee's Summit, Missouri, USA; a letter from Harry S. Truman to his wife records the purchase of cattle from 'Makin Brothers'; perhaps their ranch benefited from the funds of the Ratheram Trust.

Fig. 14 Tomb of Edward and Harriet Ratheram, Malvern Cemetery

Fig. 15 The Inscription on the Tomb of Edward and Harriet Ratheram

2.2 Harriet Frances Ratheram (St. Clare, 29th Jan 1871 to 25th Feb 1871)

Harriet Frances Ratheram, the eldest child of Charles and Harriet Ratheram was born at Kings Norton about 1825 and is recorded living with her parents on the 6th of June 1841 at The Henburys, Moseley, Kings Norton, with her brother Edward on the 30th of March 1851 at Monument Lane, Edgbaston and she came to Malvern with him in 1852; the records of her movements up to July 1870 are the same as recorded for Edward.

She was the official owner of St. Clare between the 29th of January 1871 and her death, although she was terminally ill at the time she became the owner of the property. She died at St. Clare on the 25th of February 1871, a month after her brother. Her age was recorded as 47. Her death was notified by Emma Cox, her servant, and the cause was given as 'Fibrous Tumour (cancer) over several years, Anasarca for last six months' (generalised fluid gathering in the intracellular space caused by heart failure, liver failure, renal failure, malnutrition or protein deficiency).

Harriet was buried on the 28th of February 1871 in the same grave as her brother, cemetery reference Grave Number 1797 Plot 4; this time the cost was only £1 1s (£103 at 2012 values).The headstone and tomb erected over the grave refers to both Edward and Harriet and the inscription applying to Harriet reads "Also of his dearly beloved Sister Harriet Frances Ratheram who died Feb 25 1871 aged 47 years".

Below both inscriptions is the quote from 1 Thessalonians Chapter 5 verse 10, "Who died for us that whether we wake or sleep we should live together with him".

Harriet wrote her Will only one week before her death, on the 18th of February 1871. In it she states that it revoked any previous dispositions but no reference to any other document has been found. Probate records for the 20th of March 1871 show that she left effects of under £800, (£78,400 at 2012 values) reassessed in December 1871 as under £2,000 (£196,000 at 2012 values). Her executors were Thomas Lane, Moundsley Hall, Kings Norton, William Makin, Sandfield Park, Liverpool and William Corner West M.D. Malvern. The Death Duty Register for 1871 shows that Thomas Lane paid death duty on Harriet's estate at Worcester.

Both of her servants were to receive a legacy free of duty; Annie Prince a sum of £25 (£2,450 at 2012 values) and Emma Cox a sum of £10 (£980 at 2012 values). Her jewellery and dresses were to be divided between Helen Makin, wife of her executor William Makin and Jane Hooman, spinster, of Great Malvern, who appears to have been the main beneficiary; she also received the residue of Harriet's estate, including £500 (£49,000 at 2012 values) stock in the Midland Railway Company.

In 1871 Jane Hooman, age 59, is recorded at 3 Abbey Terrace, Great Malvern, the daughter of John Hooman, a farmer of Ombersley, Worcestershire. She died at 1 Abbey Terrace, Great Malvern on the 27th of September 1880 leaving effects of under £5,000 (£500,000 at 2012 values).

The Worcester Records Office holds details of Harriet's estate: 705:550/BA4600/1054/vii. 1867 – 1871, about 13 papers relating to the estate of Harriet Ratheram of Great Malvern, deceased. Documents deposited by Marcy, Hemmingway and son, Bewdley, solicitors.

A black and white cut-out silhouette of Harriet dated 1838 was sold at Bonham's, auctioneers, San Francisco, Sale 13997, Lot 280, 24th July, 2006. The sale statement is shown below:

> Lot 280. A Framed Cut Paper Silhouette Of A Harriet Ratheram
>
> Inscribed indistinctly 5 feet 1 inch, Miss Harriet Ratheram, reverse with label inscribed
> The Henburys Moseley, Birmingham, 2d febry 1838.
>
> Height of image 8 1/4 inches (22.5cm); framed height 10 1/2 inches (26cm).
>
> Sold for $1,135 inclusive of Buyers Premium (about £680).

At the time the silhouette was made Harriet was 13 years of age. Attempts to determine the current owner of the silhouette have not been successful.

2.3 Thomas Lane (St. Clare, 25th Feb 1871 to 1872)

Thomas Lane was born in Birmingham about 1820 to Joseph Lane and his wife Sarah.

On the 6th of June 1841 they are recorded living at 3 Great Charles Street, Birmingham, Warwickshire together with three servants; both Joseph and Thomas are recorded as Goldbeaters. Around this time Thomas Lane was a business associate of Charles Ratheram with whom he is recorded in the proposed development of a railway between Wolverhampton and Worcester.

On the 6th of July 1843 at Brighton, Sussex, Thomas married Ann Perry Shaw, second daughter of Charles and Phoebe Shaw, the elder sister of Helen Elizabeth Makin nee Shaw. During the next eight years they had two daughters, both born in Edgbaston, Warwickshire.

On the 30th of March 1851 Thomas and family were living in Moseley and he was recorded as 'Merchant'; there were four servants listed. His son and heir, Charles Pelham Lane was born at the end of that year.

In 1852 Thomas bought Moundsley Hall, Kings Norton from Edward Dawson, widower of the former owner Mary Simpson. He continued to live there throughout his life being recorded there in both the 1861 and 1871 censuses. By this time he was a Magistrate for Worcester and Birmingham, Justice of the Peace, Deputy Lieutenant of the County, Land owner, Bullion dealer and Metal manufacturer employing 140 men. The number of servants had now increased to six.

On the death of Harriet Ratheram on 25th February 1871, under the terms of the Will of Edward Ratheram, Thomas Lane became the owner of St. Clare, Priory Road, Great Malvern. There is no evidence that he ever lived there.

On the 24th of November 1873, Joseph Lane died at Clifton Villa, Kings Norton; he was aged 78 and he left an estate of under £30,000 (£2,790,000 at 2012).

Two and a half years later on the 26th of May 1876, his son, Thomas Lane died at Moundsley Hall, Kings Norton leaving an estate of under £50,000 (£4,650,000 at 2012 values),

This estate passed to Charles Pelham Lane, who continued to live at Moundsley Hall until his death in 1936, after which the property was demolished revealing that the large, Victorian, brick building had encased an earlier Tudor timber framed building dating from about 1520.

No reference has been found to indicate that Charles Pelham Lane owned St. Clare, but his inheritance did include 'other properties in Warwickshire and Worcestershire' so it is not impossible.

2.4 Hon. John Henry Roper-Curzon (St. Clare, 1872 to 1886)

The Honourable John Henry Roper-Curzon was born on the 13th of February 1802 at Waterperry, Oxfordshire, to Bridget Roper-Curzon nee Hawkins, (born in London about 1772, died at Broadstairs, Kent, in November 1826) and Henry Francis Roper-Curzon, (born at Linsted, Kent, in May 1767, died in London, on the 8th of March 1842), who became 14th Baron Teynham on the death of his cousin in 1824. John Henry was baptized at St. Marylebone, Westminster on the 19th of February 1802. His parents were recorded at that time as Henry Curzon, Esquire and Bridget.

John Henry was possibly the couple's eighth child, there being some uncertainty as to the total number of children born to these parents. Public trees available on 'Ancestry.co.uk' give families ranging from 3 to 16 children; 'The Plantagenet Rolls of the Blood Royal' give only 5 names; an entry in the London Gazette of August 1844 regarding disposal of the assets of Henry Francis names 9 children and refers to a further '9 younger children'; 'Family Search' refer to a possible 15 births. The one certain thing is that John Henry was one of a very large family!

At the time of his birth his father, born Henry Francis Roper, had adopted the surname Curzon, but on the 22nd of June 1813, the Prince Regent granted him the right to add his original surname before Curzon because he was heir presumptive to the Teynham title, hence Roper-Curzon.

John Henry served as an officer in the Army with the 98th Foot Regiment. He was appointed Ensign in January 1824 and Lieutenant in June 1828. His Army career appears to have been a short one; on the 30th of December 1831 the War Office announced that Lieutenant John Henry Roper-Curzon, now of the 37th Foot Regiment, was to be retired on half pay; he would have been only 29 years old. A newspaper report in the Worcester Chronicle dated 12th of April 1886 giving details of his funeral suggests that he was involved with the Army until 1838.

On the 7th of April 1829 he married Isabella Hodgson at St. Cuthbert, Carlisle, Cumberland. She was born in Bengal on the 12th of December 1804, daughter of Colonel James Hodgson and Marie Theresa Hodgson nee Hardwick.

On the 6th of June 1841 John Henry and Isabella are recorded with five children, all born in Cumberland, living at Derwent Lodge, Crosthwaite, Cumberland; Henrietta Maria born on the 6th of March 1831; Margaret Sydney born about 1836; James Gerald born on the 10th of January 1837; Mary Matilda, or Mary Nathalia as she is recorded on her birth certificate, born on the 24th of February 1838; Richard Henry born on the 26th of January 1840.

At the time of the census John Henry is recorded as 'Independent' and employed a total of six female servants. The record does not give details of their duties. Their youngest daughter, Lucy, was born after the census on the 28th of June 1841.

It appears that John Henry had business interests in the firm known as 'Sir Richard Hodgson and Company, Common Brewers and Maltsters' of Carlisle. A notice in the London Gazette for May 1842 records the dissolution of a partnership between John Hodgson and a group of other members of this firm, including John Henry Roper-Curzon.

By the 30th of March 1851 John and Isabella had moved to St. John's Lodge, Tivoli, Cheltenham, Gloucestershire, where his occupation is given as 'Army Officer – Half Pay'. Two children are not recorded with the family – Henrietta Maria who was visiting a cousin, Rev. Robert Gutch, Vicar of Seagrave, Barrow on Soar, Leicestershire and James who was a boarder at Newick House, Cheltenham College, with Housemaster Rev. William Baxter. The other children were being educated at home. They now employed just two female servants.

On the 11th of December 1851, at Cheltenham, Henrietta Maria married Matthewman Hodgson Donald, Cotton Manufacturer born about 1823 at Wigton, Cumberland. They lived in Stanwix, Cumberland where they had five children. Henrietta Maria died on the 27th of April 1876 and Matthewman died on the 25th of December 1885, leaving effects of £14,577 5s 9d (£1,457,730 at 2012 values) resworn June 1886 as £18,590 19s (£2,045,004 at 2012 values).

On the 18th of September 1858 Isabella Roper Curzon died at Cheltenham.

The following year, in 1859 at Cheltenham, Margaret Sydney married Rev. Thomas Trafford Shipman, born about 1831 at Sedgebrook, Lincolnshire. They had four children born in Cumberland where Thomas was Rector of Rickergate and Nether Denton; they later moved to Liddiard Tregoze, Wiltshire where he was again Rector. Thomas died there on the 27th of August 1884 leaving an estate of £4,414 4s 6d (£441,420 at 2012 values) and Margaret Sydney died on the 30th of November 1887 at 2 Dover Terrace, Southsea, Hampshire leaving an estate of £423 13s (£46,601 at 2012 values).

After the death of his wife Isabella, John Henry did not stay alone for long; on the 24th of July 1860 at St. James' Parish Church, Paddington, London, he married Harriet Ann Brown born in London about 1824, the daughter of Major John Harman Brown (deceased) a former Major with the 90th Foot Regiment.

They were recorded on the 7th of April 1861 at St. John's Lodge, Tivoli, Cheltenham; John Henry was still on half pay. Mary; Richard, occupation given as 'Gent'; and Lucy were living with them and there was now only one female servant. Harriet's mother and sisters were living close by at 2 Salopian Villas, Andover Place, Cheltenham.

On the 17th of January 1863 at Cheltenham, Richard Henry married Emily Cottam Atkinson born about 1840 at Boston Spa, Yorkshire, daughter of Joseph Milner Atkinson, Landed Gentleman. They had four daughters, all born in different parts of the country including London, Cumberland and Gloucestershire.

They finally settled at St. Kitts, St. Andrews Road, Malvern, Worcestershire where Richard Henry died on the 20th of April 1924 aged 84; administration of his effects was first granted in May 1924 to Emily for £443 4s 10d (£22,162 at 2012 values) and after her death, to daughter Gertrude in 1935 for £2,004 3s 9d, (£118,248 at 2012 values). Emily died at St. Kitts, St. Andrew's Road, Malvern on the 26th of May 1934 aged 93 leaving effects of £859 13s.6d, (£50,720 at 2012 values); Gertrude died at Battle, Sussex in 1953 at the age of 83.

On the 11th of October 1863 Mary Nathalia Roper Curzon died in Cheltenham; she never married.

In 1870 at Cheltenham, Lucy married John Nanson, born about 1820 at Carlisle, Cumberland. He was an attorney and Town Clerk of Carlisle. John was a widower whose first wife Caroline died in December 1867, possibly in childbirth. With Caroline he had thirteen children, four of whom died before their 5th birthday, but only one son is ever recorded with them on census records; the other children are recorded at various boarding schools.

Only Edward James Nanson aged 19 is recorded with John and Lucy on the 2nd of April 1871. Between 1871 and 1883 Lucy gave birth to seven children but two died soon after birth. She died on the 14th of January 1889, at Carlisle, Cumberland aged 47 leaving an estate of £442 1s 3d, (£48,625 at 2012 values). John Nanson died on the 17th of September 1891 at Kendal, Westmorland aged 71; he left effects of £288 (£14,975 at 2012 values) as shown in the Probate Calendar for May 1930; no earlier record was found.

One of Lucy's children was recorded as born at Houghton House, Houghton, Cumberland, at a time when John Henry Dixon Phelps, a later resident of St. Clare, was living at Houghton Vicarage. It is not known if there is any connection between the families.

On the 2nd of April 1871 John Henry and Harriet Ann were living at 2 Portland Place, Great Malvern, possibly in rooms, since there appears to be three separate family groups recorded at the same address. John Henry was now a 'Retired Officer' and they had no servants with them. They then moved to St. Clare in August of that year. Littlebury's Directory of 1873 records John Henry, and presumably Harriet Ann, at St. Clare, none of John Henry's children ever lived there.

He was obviously involved in the life of the locality, Berrow's Worcester Journal dated the 22nd of February 1873 records that John Henry attended the Annual Meeting of subscribers to the Malvern Rural Hospital together with the Headmaster of Malvern College, Rev. A. Faber, Dr. William Corner West and a number of business men and vicars of the area.

The same year, 1873, he was listed in the parish magazine as a Governor of the Lyttleton Grammar School, Great Malvern, a connection that continued for a number of years since on the 26th of August 1882 the Worcester Chronicle reported that both John Henry and Harriet had attended the Annual Speech Day of the school where she had presented the prizes.

On the 3rd of April 1881 John Henry was recorded, with Harriet Ann, at St. Clare, as 'Retired Officer and Peer's son'. His 85 year old sister Julia d'Avigony (given as De Chevigny in London Gazette and other records) and a widowed friend were living with them. There were also two servants.

Worcester Chronicle carried a report on the 20th of March 1886 that 'John Henry Roper-Curzon is lying dangerously ill at Malvern. Sir William Gull is in attendance and little hope is entertained for his recovery.'

John Henry died at St. Clare on the 2nd of April 1886. Newspaper reports in both the Worcester Chronicle for the 12th of April 1886 and Berrow's Worcester Journal for the 17th of April, give details of his funeral at 'the Cemetery' Malvern on Saturday, the 10th of April. The service was conducted by the vicar of the Priory Church, Rev. Isaac Gregory Smith, and the choir of the Priory 'led the procession from the chapel to the grave'; he was buried in grave number 1223, plot 3.

The grave lies immediately behind that of Jenny Lind and the large plot is marked by a grey marble cross, now laid down for safety reasons. The inscription, which is not inscribed but appears to have been etched into the marble, is worn and extremely difficult to read.

In his will, proved at Worcester on the 22nd of July 1886, he left a Personal Estate of £1,506 19s 1d (£165,764 at 2012 values). Harriet Ann Roper Curzon, widow and relict, was the sole executrix. The Death Duty Register shows that Harriet paid death duty on John Henry's estate at Worcester.

Fig. 16 The Burial Plot of the Roper-Curzon Family, Malvern Cemetery

2.5 Harriet Ann Roper-Curzon nee Brown (St. Clare, 2nd April 1886 to Sept 1888)

Harriet Ann Brown was born about 1824 in London, the eldest of six children, two boys and four girls. Her parents were John Harman Brown, a Major of Her Majesty's 90th Foot Regiment, born about 1784 in Warminster, Wiltshire and Ann, born about 1801 in Wimbledon, Surrey.

The only record found for her before her marriage to John Henry Roper-Curzon is the census entry of the 30th of March 1851. She was recorded as visiting the Rev. Thomas Charles Griffith, age 32, born at Cam, Gloucestershire, his wife Elizabeth and their young family, at The Rectory, Whittington, Northleach, Gloucestershire; she was described as 'gentlewoman income unknown'.

At the time her parents were living at 2 Salopian Villas, Andover Place, Cheltenham. Her father died there in December 1855 aged 90 but her mother continued to live there until her death on the 19th of May 1884 aged 84. This house was very close to the first home that Harriet shared with John Henry after their marriage.

She married John Henry on the 24th of July 1860 at St. James's Church, Paddington, London and is recorded with him in Cheltenham and Malvern until his death on the 2nd of April 1886.

Harriet Ann remained at St. Clare until the 22nd of September 1888, as recorded in the Malvern Advertiser; she is also listed there in Kelly's Directory for 1888.

Harriet Ann came from a family with strong military connections; in addition to her father, two of her brothers served as officers with the Indian Army and her sister Lucy Maria was married to a retired General, so it is possible that the next occupants of St. Clare, Major General Henry Imlach Bett and family, were already known to her.

Harriet Ann moved to 5 The Lees, Firs Estate, Great Malvern where she was recorded on the 5th of April 1891 with one servant. The following year, at Malvern, she became the second wife of the widowed Rev. Thomas Charles Griffith, and moved to his home at St. Matthew's Rectory, Kingsdown Road, Surbiton, Surrey where they were recorded on the 31st of March 1901.

At some point after this they moved to 6 Oxford Road, Cheltenham, Gloucestershire, where Thomas died on the 29th of November 1903 leaving £6,224 19s, (£622,495 at 2012 values). Harriet Ann was not mentioned in the grant of Probate.

After Thomas' death she moved to her family home of 2 Salopian Villas, Tivoli Road, Cheltenham, Gloucestershire to live with her sister Adelaide Keith Brown and her companion Alice Mary Austin.

She died there on the 26th of March 1907 leaving £145 19s 11d, (£14,600 at 2012 values). Probate was granted on the 20th of April 1907 to Adelaide Keith Brown, Spinster, who herself died on the 14th of May 1909 leaving £1,664 11s 10d (£163,161 at 2012 values) to Alice Mary Austin and Frederick Lennox Harman Brown, Surgeon, (son of her brother Major John Frederick Harman Brown deceased).

Harriet Ann was buried in Malvern Cemetery, Madresfield Road, Malvern, Worcestershire in the same grave 1223 Plot 3 as her first husband John Henry Roper-Curzon. There is an inscription on the base of the cross which is partly obscured due to the laid down cross being placed above it. It reads "Harriet Ann, widow of Honble (sic) John Henry Roper-Curzon and secondly of the Rev. T.C. Griffith and daughter of the Late Major John Harman Brown JP and DL of Sal……. Formerly of HM Regt and ADC…….".

As no children were ever recorded with them it came as a surprise to find that there is an inscription on the grave surround stating 'and all infant children of Hon. John Henry and Harriet Ann Roper-Curzon'. A search of the Birth, Marriages and Deaths Index has shown one possible recorded birth at Cheltenham of an Alfred G M Roper-Curzon in the last quarter of 1866 followed by a death in the second quarter of 1867.

No unidentified Roper-Curzon births or deaths have been found between 1860 and 1880. Since the inscription suggests that there were a number of infants buried it must be assumed that any other children were stillborn.

Fig. 17 The Inscription for Harriet Ann Roper Curzon

Fig.18 Inscription in Grave Surround

2.6 Major General Henry Imlach Bett (St. Clare, 1890 to 1894)

Henry Imlach Bett was born at Coupar Angus, Perth, Scotland where his baptism is recorded on the 2nd of September 1826. His father was William Bett, born about 1776 at Coupar Angus, Perth, recorded as 'Merchant in Wine (or Mine) Company' on the baptism record, but later was an 'Agent for the Linen Bank of Scotland'; his mother was Janet Smith Bett nee Johnstone born about 1801 at Blairgowrie, Perth.

Henry was a professional soldier serving in India and military records show that on the 5th of March 1844 he was appointed to the 42nd Regiment Native Infantry. He was at Cuttack Station, Madras, East Indies and in January 1853 was ordered to Jubbulpore. The London Gazette and Edinburgh Gazette records show that he was promoted to Lieutenant on the 15th of November 1853. Between June and August 1858 he served in the field at Raichore Doab for 2 months. He was promoted to Captain with the Madras Staff Corps on the 5th of March 1859; on the 6th of March 1864 he was made Major and he became Lieutenant Colonel on the 5th of March 1870.

He returned to England briefly that year and on the 31st of August 1870, at the Parish Church of Whiteparish, Wiltshire, he married Lavinia Georgine Bourdillon, born on the 7th of February 1844 at St. Pancras, London and baptized at St. Mary's, Hornsey, Middlesex on the 24th of June 1844. She was the daughter of Stafford Bourdillon, Solicitor, and Amelia Anne Augusta Bourdillon nee Faulkener, of Whiteparish, Wiltshire, both of whom died at Stockbridge, Hampshire in 1898 aged 84 and 82 respectively.

Henry's address at the time of his marriage was given on the marriage certificate as New Hall, Kettins, Scotland; this proved to be the home of his younger brother, David Inches Bett as recorded on the 1871 census for Scotland.

Henry returned to Madras with Lavinia, and their first child Jessie Amelia Bett was born there about 1873. It is not clear exactly when Henry returned to Wiltshire, but Lavinia returned before the birth of Stafford Henry Imlach Bett on the 1st of August 1874 at Whiteparish, Wiltshire. Her parents were recorded in the area of Whiteparish in the 1871 census so she may well have been living with them at that time.

On the 5th of March 1875 Henry was promoted to Colonel, having served the qualifying period as Lieutenant Colonel, and on the 5th of June 1875 he was given the honorary rank of Major General to mark his retirement from military service.

A second son, Francis Bourdillon Bett, was born on the 31st of July 1876 at Figheldean, Wiltshire, where he was christened on the 1st of October 1876. The family then moved to Holtye House, Hartfield, Sussex where Margaret Lavinia Bett was born on the 2nd of March 1879, followed by Elspeth Marion Bett on the 31st of December 1880.

On the 3rd of April 1881 Henry, (now described as 'Major General (retd.) Madras Staff Corps') and Lavinia were living at Holtye House with their five children. Lavinia's parents, Stafford and Amelia Bourdillon were recorded as visitors. They employed five servants including a Governess, Nurse, Under-nurse, Cook and House maid.

On or about the 26th of April 1890, the family moved to St. Clare, Priory Road, Great Malvern where they are recorded in the census taken on the 5th of April. The children are all 'Scholars' and there are three servants - Nurse, Cook and Parlour maid. They are also recorded there in the 1892 Kelly's Directory, but their stay at St. Clare lasted only until July 1894 when they moved, most likely to Pilstone House, Llandogo, Monmouth, where Henry, Lavinia and daughters Jessie, Margaret Lavinia and Elspeth were recorded on the 31st of March 1901, together with five servants - Nurse, Cook, Parlour maid and House Maid.

On the 22nd of July 1902 daughter Margaret Lavinia died in the River Wye aged 22. An inquest by Bickerton H. Deakin, Coroner for Monmouth, held on the 25th of July 1902, recorded a verdict of 'Accidental drowning' and the death was registered on the 28th of July 1902. A report in the Bath Chronicle and Weekly Gazette states that she 'died accidently in the River Wye while picking flowers'. It appears from Googlemaps that Pilstone House and its estate at Llandogo is situated close to the bank of the River Wye.

Henry Imlach died on the 7th of May 1904 at Gibraltar House, Monmouth; it is likely that this was then the family home. Henry left effects of £36,187 (£3,618,700 at 2012 values) and probate was granted to Lavinia.

Early passenger records for foreign journeys are poorly recorded, with only the minimum information being given, which makes it difficult to be sure that the correct records have been found. However, on the 19th of October 1904 Mrs Lavinia Bett, born 1844, left London on a passage aboard SS Johannesburg bound for Capetown, South Africa, most likely visiting her son Francis.

It is not known when she returned but there is a record for a 'Mrs Bett' (no age given) on SS Goorka in February 1905 from Natal to Southampton; without further details it cannot be proved to be Lavinia. It is possible that Elspeth also visited South Africa at that time, but with no identification other than 'Miss Bett' being recorded, it is again 'likely' rather than 'proven'.

On the 13th of August 1909, Miss E. M. Bett, believed to be Elspeth Marion Bett age 28, a student, is recorded on board SS Empress of Ireland leaving Liverpool for Quebec, Canada. No further details are given so it is not known where she disembarked, and no identifiable return journey was found.

There was no record for Lavinia or Elspeth in the 1911 UK census but they arrived at Southampton from Algiers on the 8th of June 1911 aboard SS Prinz Ludwig. Again no identifiable records could be found for the outward journey, but Miss Elspeth Bett left Southampton aboard the SS Prinzess Alice on the 26th of September 1911 to return to Algiers.

On the 30th of November 1911 Elspeth died at Villa Aicha, Algiers. Her death was registered as Elizabeth M. Bett in the GRO Consular Death Index 1911-1915, Algiers; she was 30 years old. The Probate Calendar entry dated 14th of February 1912 gave her address as 'Gibraltar', Monmouth. Probate was granted to her Solicitor and Bank manager and she left an estate of £21,554 14s 1d (£2,090,806 at 2012 values). No beneficiaries were named.

On the 16th of January 1914 Lavinia died at 14 Thurloe Court, Kensington, London. The Probate Calendar gave her place of residence as Gibraltar, Monmouthshire and probate was granted to her Solicitors and her son Stafford, leaving effects of £1,045 17s 2d, (£98,310 at 2012 values)

Jessie Amelia Bett was not found on the 1911 census. On the 28th of April 1921, age 49, she died at Brislington House Lunatic Asylum, nr. Bristol, the earliest purpose built, and privately owned asylum, dating from 1804. Originally developed by Dr Edward Fox, a Quaker, and continually owned by the Fox family until at least 1951, it is now known as 'Brislington Nursing Home'. Brislington was not solely intended for Quakers but "was mainly for people who could afford (and wished) to pay for their relatives to be confined in good conditions."

Whether Jessie had been confined there at other times is not known; the censuses for Brislington House have been checked, without success. She was listed neither as patient nor staff in 1891; in 1911 she was not listed amongst the staff, and patients were recorded only by their initials making it impossible to know who they were.

On the 16th of August 1921 probate for Jessie was granted to Stafford Imlach Bett, fruit farmer, and effects amounted to £22,613 4s (£836,688 at 2012 values)

Stafford Henry Imlach Bett was not found in the 1901 or 1911 censuses, but he arrived in Southampton from Capetown, South Africa on the 21st of April 1901 aboard SS Danube; Later the same year, on the 2nd of October, he left London bound for Capetown, South Africa aboard SS Johannesburg. His occupation was given as 'Farmer' but no further details are available.

On the 24th of April 1912 he married Margaret Archdale, (born at Aylsham, Norfolk in 1873), daughter of Charles Wells Archdale,(formerly Charles Wells Hogge, born Biggleswade 1833) former Captain with the 85th Light Infantry and Captain of Norfolk Volunteers, and his wife Emelia Jane Bagge, daughter of William Bagge 1st Baronet Bagge of Stradsett, Conservative MP for West Norfolk.

They went on to live at Thornham Cottage, Thornham, Kings Lynn, Norfolk, where Stafford was farming and this was the family home for many years. A son, Henry Bourdillon Imlach Bett was born on the 22nd of May 1913, registered at Evesham, Worcestershire, and a daughter Pleasance Margaret Bett was born at Thornham in 1915.

The same year, at the age of 40, Stafford enlisted with the Army Service Corps and during WW1 served as an Ambulance driver in France. He was badly wounded and his left leg was amputated below the knee. After a period in hospital and at Roehampton he was finally discharged as unfit for further military service in 1919 and returned to Thornham.

In February 1925 he is recorded on a passage bound for Capetown aboard SS Ascanius, accompanied by his brother Francis who was farming in Rhodesia. He is recorded as 'Landowner' of Thornham, Norfolk; he returned alone on the same vessel arriving at Liverpool on the 25th of June 1925.

Stafford died at Thornham Cottage, Thornham, Norfolk, on the 27th of April 1944 aged 70 leaving an estate of £25,830 6s 3d (£955,732 at 2012 values). His wife Margaret died at Silfield Nursing Home, Hunstanton, Norfolk on the 25th of May 1961 aged 88. She left an estate of £85,350 10s 6d (£1,621.660 at 2012 values)

Francis Bourdillon Bett was not found on the UK censuses for 1901 or 1911 but it appears that he was probably farming in South Africa at the time; it is likely that Stafford was visiting him in 1901, as was his widowed mother in 1904.

He seems to have spent much of his time travelling back and forth between the UK and South Africa with trips to Canada thrown in as well. Between 1911 and 1936 there are 19 entries in Passenger lists, both inward and outward, between UK and Capetown, South Africa at intervals of 2 or 3 years. He stayed at Thornham Cottage, the home of his brother Stafford, when in the UK, sometimes for up to 6 months, before returning to Rhodesia. His occupation is most frequently recorded as farmer or rancher but in 1920 he is recorded as 'Civil Servant' and in 1925 and 1931 as 'Landowner'.

In August 1934 he was accompanied on the passage from Natal to Southampton, en route for Thornham, by his niece Pleasance Margaret Bett age 19, daughter of Stafford and Emilia. Her brother, Henry Bourdillon Bett age 22, recorded as farmer of Thornham, Norfolk, was with him on the passage to Liverpool from Durban in

May 1936. Presumably they had been out to visit him at his farm. On the 29th of September 1936 he made what appears to have been his last journey from Southampton to South Africa, alone, aboard the SS Athlone Castle.

Francis died in St George's Nursing Home, Bullawayo, Southern Rhodesia on the 30th of March 1937 age 61. Probate records for the 17th of January 1938 show that he left assets of £1,962 10s.6d (£113,825 at 2012 values) in England and administration was granted to his attorney Lewis Loftus Baker and two others; no members of the family are named and no indication of the beneficiaries is given.

Cecil John Rhodes Pioneer Column only arrived in South Africa in 1890 and subsequent immigration of white colonists was fairly slow; Francis Bourdillon Bett must have been amongst the early settlers of that country if he was already there in 1901 when Stafford is recorded visiting South Africa.

There is no record of a marriage for Francis; he was never accompanied by a spouse on his many journeys, and searches have not revealed any other information. It was rather surprising, and most likely no more than a coincidence, that while searching for 'Francis Bett, Rhodesia', a photograph was found in 'The Standard (Online Edition)' published in Nairobi, Kenya, 18th of May 2011, showing Francis Bett, Roads Minister, examining a pineapple!

2.7 Dr. Charles Harry Hanger East (St. Clare, 1894 to 1921)

Charles Harry Hanger East was born on the 12th of September 1861 at Kettering, Northamptonshire to Emma East nee Hanger (born about 1825 at Kettering) and Charles East (born about 1822 at Kettering). Charles Harry was the youngest of four children.

At the time of his birth his father was employed as a traveller in the shoe trade, having been recorded as a 'Clicker' in the census of the 30th of March 1951. He had married Emma Hanger at Kettering, in December 1847 and, around that time, set up his own shoe manufacturing business that by 1871 was employing 115 men at the Britannia Works of East and Co. He died at Kettering on the 16th of October 1875 aged 52, leaving an estate of under £14,000 (£1,302,000 at 2012 values) to Emma. She continued to live in Kettering and died there on the 7th of September 1906 age 82; she left effects of £3,443 16s 11d (£344,385 at 2012 values) to her three sons.

Between 1880 and 1890 Charles Harry studied Medicine at Durham University and Kings' College, London, taking L.S.A in 1884; M.R.C.S. 1886; M.B. and B.S. 1887; M.D. 1890. From 1890 he practised at Kings' College Hospital, London where he was House Surgeon to Lord Lister, medical registrar and tutor, and also assistant demonstrator in Anatomy. Some of his annotated notebooks are kept in the Hospital Archives.

While at Kings' College Hospital he met Amy Rynd, daughter of Rev. Henry Nassau Rynd and Elizabeth Rynd nee Kennedy; she was working as a nurse at the time. Family records say 'Amy was said to be stunningly beautiful'. She was born on the 28th of August 1863 at The Wilderness, Box, Wiltshire, and brought up at the Vicarage in Shinfield Green, Berkshire where her father was vicar; she was the eighth of ten children, eight girls and two boys. Charles and Amy married on the 1st of November 1890 at St. Matthew's Church, Bayswater, London.

The medical register for 1891 records Charles Harry at Pontrilas Herefordshire. This address was also recorded on the marriage certificate but on the 5th of April 1891 their address is given as Belgrave, Cupids Hill, Grosmont, Herefordshire; Charles Harry is recorded as a General Practitioner at this time. There is one servant recorded, Mary Mitchell age 22, General Domestic, born Kingston Surrey.

The exact date for their move to Malvern is not known but Charles and Amy's first child, Charles Frederick Terence East, known as Terence, was born at Enderley, 10 Avenue Road, Great Malvern on the 20th of June 1894.

In the 1891 census this was a multi-occupied property and it is likely that they were living in only part of the house. Enderley was also the registered address for the practice of Barkley and Holme, Dental Surgeons as recorded in the Kelly's Directories for 1892 and 1900. It was later used as the sick bay for 'Lawnside' boarding school.

Charles and Amy moved to St. Clare, Priory Road, Malvern, four months after Terence was born, although the Medical Register for 1895 still gives Charles' address as Enderley, Great Malvern. Their second child Norah Kathleen Meliora East was born on the 25th of November 1895 at St. Clare, where both children are recorded with their parents on the 31st of March 1901, together with three servants including Mary Mitchell as Nurse, a Cook and a Housemaid.

Kelly's Directory for 1900 shows that Charles Harry was involved in both general medical practice and acting as a surgeon at Malvern Rural Hospital, Newtown and in the Directory for 1912 he is recorded at Malvern Community Hospital, Lansdowne Crescent which was opened in May 1911. As Charles Harry is listed at St. Clare in the

Commercial section of both Directories it is believed that he had consulting rooms at the house for his general practice.

Between 1901 and 1911 Terence was educated as a boarder at Wells Court Prep School, Tewkesbury and Wells Prep School, Malvern Wells and by the 2nd of April 1911 both children were at boarding school; Terence at Winchester College, Hampshire where his housemaster was Charles William Little, and Norah at Wycombe Abbey School, Marlow Hill, High Wycombe, Hertfordshire where her housemistress at Campbell House was Ann Maria Mary Scott from Australia. Terence was President of the Boat Club during his time at Winchester.

At St. Clare on the 2nd of April 1911, Charles and Amy are recorded together with Amy's sister Constance and Sick Nurse, Bertha Wilkins. There were also three servants; Mary Mitchell was now Cook-Housekeeper, with a House-Parlour maid and Kitchen maid. It is believed that Amy was ill with tuberculosis at this time which explains the presence of the Sick Nurse and could be another reason why the children were not at St. Clare.

Amy died on the 21st of December 1911 at the age of 48. She was buried on the 23rd of December 1911 in Malvern Cemetery, Madresfield Road, Malvern, Plot No 4CP 2623. The plot is marked by a large Celtic style decorated cross which has been laid down for safety reasons. The lettering of the inscription is in lead which was pinned to the stone but is beginning to break away; it is still possible to read the name and date of death and the words "We will remember thy love".

Probate was granted to Charles Harry for effects of £608 15s. 11d (£59,054 at 2012 values)

Charles Harry continued to live at St. Clare and continued in general practise and at Malvern Community Hospital; 'East family hearsay' suggests that he treated Elgar and a record of him being called to the Elgar household when their daughter Carice was ill with whooping cough has been found in one of Elgar's diaries reproduced on the Internet.

On the 16th of March 1916 Charles Harry married Mabel Gray Momber nee Barker. Mabel was daughter of Christopher Dove Barker, Ship owner and Banker from North Shields, Co. Durham, local magistrate for Malvern and member of Malvern College Council, and his wife Alice Gray Barker nee Elmslie. Mabel was born on the 4th of January 1868 at Radnor House, College Road, Malvern, the eighth of ten children, seven girls and three boys. On the 2nd of April 1871, the census records Mabel with her parents and siblings at Radnor House, together with a total of nine servants. Radnor House is now the No. 8 Girls Boarding House for Malvern College having been bought by the College in 1906 following the death of C. D. Barker.

Mabel was educated at Mistrey Girls Boarding School, Cambridge House, Main Road, Hanley Swan, where she was recorded on the 3rd of April 1881, and in 1887 she married Gustavus Albert Momber. On the 5th of April 1891 they are recorded as living in Berkeley, Gloucestershire with a son Rex age 1 year.

Rex was born Albert Reginald Theodore Momber on the 1st of May 1889 at Cleveland House, Priory Road Great Malvern. At the time Cleveland House was run as a lodging house by Charles Ellis. Rex died in Cambridge in 1911, aged 22 and a number of Institutions benefitted from his estate, including the National Marine Biology Association who received a bequest of £1,100 (£26,400 at 2012 values) in 1953-1954 as recorded on the MBA website.

Mabel had been widowed in 1910 when Lieutenant Colonel Gustavus Albert Momber died in St. Remo Italy; the death was registered at the British Consulate for the area.

At the time that Charles Harry and Mabel married in 1916, the residents of St. Ronan's, next door to St. Clare, included Mabel's sister Lily Adeline and her husband Arthur James Wharry, a Surgeon, as recorded in the Medical Registers of 1911-1919, although the 1911 census records only two servants present at St. Ronan's. It is believed that Alice Gray Barker nee Elmslie, mother of Mabel and Lily Adeline was also living at St. Ronan's from at least 1908, when Kelly's Directory of private residents lists 'Mrs C. D. Barker' at that address.

However, Malvern College records show that 'in 1906 following the death of C. D. Barker, a member of College Council, Radnor House was empty, so it is likely that she moved to St. Ronan's at that time. Although not present at the time of the census on the 2nd of April 1911 she is again recorded there in Kelly's Directory for 1912. She died at St. Ronan's on the 27th of February 1918 leaving effects of £2,757 14s 3d (£157,189 at 2012 values).

Charles Harry retired in 1921, and moved to the villa at St. Junia, St. Remo, Italy. An entry in a personal notebook belonging to Terence East states that St. Clare was 'given up' in 1920; similar entries relating to other properties refer to them as being 'sold', which leaves it open to question as to whether or not Charles Harry East had actually owned St. Clare.

Charles and Mabel lived at St. Remo until between 1927 and 1931 when the Medical register shows their address as 'Birchwood', Malvern. At some time after 1935 they moved to 'The Beeches', Guilford Road, Bagshot, Surrey, where Charles Harry died on the 22nd of December 1945 aged 84. Probate records give his address as The Beeches Bagshot, Surrey, care of Lloyds Bank Ltd, Malvern Worcestershire and probate was granted at Llandudno on the 13th of March 1946 to the bank and Terence East for effects amounting to £10,722 17s 1d (£375,300 at 2012 values).

Charles Harry is recorded on the same headstone as Amy in Malvern Cemetery, Plot No 4CP 2623, but the Council have no written record of a date of burial. The only additional inscription is that of his name and date of death.

Mabel died at 'Five Trees Nursing Home, Sunninghill, Ascot, Berkshire on the 17th of March 1950 aged 82. Probate was granted at London on the 14th of September 1950 to her niece Elaine Maud Colmore, widow, and John Bernard Watson Lambert, solicitor for effects of £8,750 10s (£253,764 at 2012 values).

Fig. 19 The Burial Plot of the East Family, Malvern Cemetery

Fig. 20 The Inscription for the East Family

After his mother's death in 1911 Terence East began his studies at New College Oxford but these were interrupted by the onset of WW1. From 1915 to 1918 he served as a Lieutenant in the Northamptonshire Regiment, being seriously wounded at Loos in 1915 and again at Arras on the 3rd of May 1917. He was also slightly wounded on the Somme in 1918. Apparently the shrapnel which was removed from his leg was displayed on the mantelpiece at home!

When he was demobbed in 1918 he resumed his studies at Oxford and graduated B.A in 1919, winning the Welch prize and M.A in 1921. He was awarded a Burney Yeo Scholarship to Kings' College Hospital Medical School in 1919. He graduated B.M. and B.Chir. in 1921, and became M.R.C.P. in 1922, being awarded a Murchison Scholarship by the Royal College of Physicians.

House appointments at Kings' College Hospital were followed by a number of prestigious appointments including in 1923 medical registrar; 1924 Radcliffe Travelling Fellow, University College Oxford; also in 1924 he became junior physician, senior medical tutor, lecturer in morbid anatomy and curator of the museum of Kings College Hospital; in 1927 he became F.R.C.P.

He was an eminent cardiologist, taking over the cardiology department at Kings' College on the retirement of Dr. Wiltshire in 1924, eventually becoming senior physician and director of the medical school in 1945. He also held a number of consultancy posts; was a member of the council of Royal College of Physicians; an examiner for Oxford University and associate editor of British Heart Journal from 1950 to 1954. He gave numerous lectures and wrote a definitive book on the 'Story of Heart Disease'.

Medical Registers for 1931 to 1943 record various London addresses for Terence, including 16 Harley Place and 66 Wimpole Street which was bombed in 1941. Details of all his addresses and other more personal information about his family life are recorded in a notebook in the possession of the family.

Terence married Muriel Leticia Luise Stein, (born on the 1st of February 1903, at Weybridge, Surrey) eldest daughter of Julius William Stein and Clara L. Stein nee Leisten, on the 15th of November 1924 at the Queens' Chapel of the Savoy dedicated to St. John the Baptist, off The Strand in London.

This is an interesting chapel being originally built in mediaeval times as part of the Savoy Palace, later known as the Savoy Hospital. It has always been a royal chapel and as such belongs to the Monarch as part of the Duchy of Lancaster. In the 18th century it had a dubious reputation as being a place for illegal marriages without banns, but in 1937 it was made the chapel for the Royal Victorian Order.

Terence's address at the time was given on the marriage certificate as 'The Precinct of the Savoy' also known as the 'Liberty of the Savoy', an area within Westminster which, until the 19th century, was governed by its own laws under the authority of the Duke of Lancaster; debtors, for example, could live in the area without the fear of arrest by the representatives of the Law.

A daughter, who is still alive in Canada today (November 2011), was born to them at Hampstead in 1927. Muriel had a number of health problems and she is reported as going abroad to recuperate. The relationship between her and Terence was not to last; they separated in 1936. From Passenger records on Ancestry.com it appears that Muriel worked in the hotel industry, her place of residence being variously given as Australia, New Zealand and Fiji. She died in September 1994 at Worthing, West Sussex, aged 91.

Terence formed a firm relationship with Zoe Beatrice Stein, younger sister of Muriel, born on the 12th of November 1911, at Chertsey,

Surrey. Together they brought up two adopted sons, one of whom is still alive, as well as Terence's daughter who was with them much of the time. Correspondence with the daughter of Jonathan Simon East is the source of the personal information on the East family. Jonathan Simon was born on the 18th of June 1942 and adopted by Terence on the 28th of August that year; he died in July 2010.

Muriel and Zoe Stein were sisters of Hans Eric Stein, father of chef Rick Stein, well known for his TV programmes, his four restaurants and cookery school in Padstow, a public house in St Merryn, and fish and chip shop in Falmouth.

In 1942 Terence and Zoe lived at 8 Upper Wimpole Street, London, then briefly in Buckinghamshire, before moving in 1945 to 4 The Grange, Wimbledon, near the Common - a house which belonged to Zoe - where they lived until 1958 when retirement saw Terence and his family move to his final home 'Gulland', St. Merryn, Cornwall where he could enjoy botany, bird-watching and sailing 'Bonxie', one of his boats.

In January 1966 Terence and Zoe were married, just 18 months before his sudden death on the 27th of August 1967 aged 73. The marriage laws in the UK did not allow marriage between a man and his sister in law, unless the first spouse was dead, until the Marriage Act of 1960 allowed divorcees the same rights as widowers. Zoe died in Bodmin, Cornwall on the 23rd of April 2000 aged 88.

Terence had a lasting love for the Malvern Hills and his family have a seat dedicated to his memory which they visit whenever they are in the area. It is sited on the path between the Wyche Cutting and Holy Well, which passes close by the boarding house for Wells Prep School where he was educated.

Norah Kathleen Meliora East was married on the 10th May 1922 at St. Paul's Church, Knightsbridge, London to Captain Waldene Edgar

Bredin, Royal Irish Regiment. He was born at Clonmel, Tipperary, Ireland in February 1893. He was the son of Major Waldene Fitzwilliam Hutchison Bredin, Royal Irish Regiment and Elizabeth Sarah Cooper Bredin nee Chadwick . Norah and Waldene lived in Weymouth and their only child Norah Elizabeth P Bredin was born there on the 14th of November 1922.

Captain Bredin served in Administrative and Special Duties Branch with the rank of Flight Lieutenant during WW2. No definite record of where they lived at this time has been found but it seems likely that it was somewhere in Surrey; Norah Elizabeth was married in Surrey North Eastern in 1956 and Waldene E Bredin died in Surrey Northern in 1961. Norah Bredin nee East, died at Poole, Dorset in July 1990 aged 94. Norah Elizabeth died in North Dorset in July 1999 aged 77.

2.8 Dr. John Henry Dixon Phelps (St. Clare, 1922 to 1934)

John Henry Dixon Phelps was born at Houghton, Carlisle, Cumberland on the 4th of January 1872, the second child and eldest son of Rev. John Phelps, (born at Wilton, Wiltshire about 1834; his christening was recorded at St. Mary's Church Wilton on the 29th of August 1834; he died between 1891 - 1901, no death record found) and Sarah Maria Dixon, (born at Houghton Hall, Carlisle, Cumberland about 1846; her christening is recorded at Houghton on the 17th of April 1846. She died on the 26th of April 1922 age 76, at 7 Caldew Street, Silloth, Cumberland, leaving £109 4s 6d (£4,368 at 2012 values).

At the time John Henry was born his father had been vicar of Houghton since 1864 and appears to have continued in that position, living at Houghton Vicarage, Stanwix, Cumberland, until his death.

There was a long tradition in the Phelps' family of service to the Church following an Oxbridge education, some combining parish work with education. There are at least 10 ordained ministers in four generations of Phelps', serving in parishes in many different areas of the country.

The most auspicious member of the family was John Henry's great grand uncle, William Whitmarsh Phelps, who at the time John Henry's father was vicar of Houghton, Carlisle, was serving as Archdeacon for the Carlisle Diocese, after having been a Housemaster at Harrow School, and about whom a number of books have been written. Only two other members of the family appear to have entered the medical profession.

John Henry was educated at Carlisle Grammar School where he was nominated and approved for a Thomas Exhibition to Queens College Oxford where he studied from 1891, obtaining the Conjoint English diploma in 1899. His clinical studies were undertaken at St. George's

Hospital, London where he held junior appointments becoming L.R.C.P (Lond) in 1899 and graduating B.M.; B.Ch. and M.R.C.S. (Eng) in 1901.

In 1903 he went to South America for three years where he served as Resident Medical Officer at the British Hospital in Buenos Aires, Argentina before returning to England and setting up in general practice near Richmond, Yorkshire where he was based for the next 17 years, also holding several public appointments. Medical Registers show his address as Catterick, Yorkshire in 1907 when he became a member of the BMA and also of the Medical Officers of Schools Association.

On the 11th of April 1907 at Lapworth Parish Church, Lapworth, Warwickshire, John Henry married Lucy Olive Parker who was born on the 8th of June 1882 at 180, Hagley Road, Edgbaston, Warwickshire to Reginald Parker, (born at Canonbury, London in 1846, died Malvern, Worcestershire in 1911), and Margaret Irving van Wart, (born Edgbaston 1855, died Orwell Lodge, Woodshears Road, Great Malvern, on the 3rd of April 1936 aged 81, leaving effects of £29,098 17s 10d (£1,687,730 at 2012 values).

Margaret van Wart was of American descent and the name Irving derives from her grandmother Sarah Irving, who was sister to Washington Irving, American author of 'Rumpelstiltskin' and the 'Legend of Sleepy Hollow', which he is reputed to have written at the van Wart's Edgbaston home for the amusement of his nephews and nieces. The name is perpetuated in the descendants of John Henry Phelps.

On the 5th of February 1909 the first son of John Henry and Lucy Peter Horsley Phelps, was born in Malvern Link, Worcestershire; the family home was in Catterick, Yorkshire at that time but Peter was born at his grandparent's home. The name Horsley links back several generations to the great grandmother of Reginald Parker, Peter's maternal grandfather.

About 1910 they left Catterick and moved to Scorton, Darlington, Yorkshire, where their second son Anthony Irving Phelps was born on the 4th of January 1911; on the 2nd of April 1911 he was recorded with his mother and brother visiting his grandparents at 'The White House', Malvern Link. John Henry is recorded as Physician and Surgeon 'on own account', at the family home in Scorton, together with the Housekeeper, Elizabeth Collingwood.

A third son, John Reginald Phelps, was born in Richmond, Yorkshire on the 31st of May 1913. Lucy and the three boys continued to live in Scorton, but for the duration of WW1 John Henry served in the R.A.M.C., with the temporary rank of Captain, at Valetta Hospital, Malta. Medical registers, however, still recorded his practise address as Scorton 1915-1919.

About 1920 John Henry came to Malvern Community Hospital and moved to St. Clare (Tel. No. Malvern 7) after Charles East in 1921.The family lived there until 1935 when they moved to Millbrook, Albert Road South, Great Malvern. He continued in general practice with the partnership Phelps, Devereux and Bishop (Tel. No. Malvern 7), as recorded in Kelly's Directory, Commercial entries for 1940. 'Devereux' is believed to refer to Arthur C. Devereux M.B.; Ch.B. (Edin.); F.R.S.C. (Eng.), Physician and Surgeon, of Howard Lodge, Avenue Road, Great Malvern.

John Henry Dixon Phelps died at Millbrook, Albert Road South on the 29th of September 1946 aged 74 leaving effects of £27,774 1s 9d (£972,093 at 2012 values) as recorded in the National Probate Calendar. Probate was granted on the 18th of March 1947 to his sons, Peter Horsley Phelps, described as 'religious worker' and John Reginald Phelps described as 'Works Manager'.

He was buried in St, James' Church Cemetery, West Malvern where he is commemorated on a headstone which includes Reginald Parker, father in law; Margaret Irving Parker, mother in law; Reginald Irving Parker, brother in law; and Rev Archibald Francis Robson, former vicar of St James', brother in law

Lucy Olive Phelps continued to live at Millbrook, as recorded in telephone directories 1946-1968, until her death on the 9th of January 1969 aged 86. She was buried in St. James' Church Cemetery, West Malvern on the 13th of January 1969. Her name is recorded on a headstone together with that of her sister, Dorothy Ann Robson, nee Parker, wife of Rev. Archibald Robson.

Peter Horsley Phelps was educated at Felsted Boarding School, nr. Dunmow, Essex where he was elected to a New Foundation Jodrell Scholarship for Classics at Oxford University on the 1st of April 1927; like his father he studied at Queens College.

The Worcester Country Cricket Club Archive records that Peter Phelps played for the county as a 'right hand batsman and bowler' and Old Felstedians record him as a 'cricketer' in their 'notable sportsmen' archive. The Worcester records show he had a very short first class career during the 1931-32 season only, playing only three matches with modest results; he made 25 runs in 4 innings. The names of both of his brothers are included in the archive report but there is no record of them having played for the county.

On the 10th of March 1934 aged 25, he left Southampton aboard SS Europa bound for New York with the 'Oxford Group'; his address was given as St. Clare Malvern. On the return journey aboard SS Empress of Australia arriving at Southampton on the 28th of June 1934 his intended place of residence was given as c/o Brown's Hotel, Dover Street, London along with several others listed as belonging to the Oxford Group; no reason for the visit to New York was given.

His occupation is unknown but Worcester C.C. Archive records that during WW2 Peter Phelps served with the National Fire Service in London and the probate records for his father in 1947 refer to him as a 'religious worker'.

On the 28th July 1945 at Christ Church, Down Street, London, Peter Horsley Phelps married Monica Denison Smith, born on the 25th of September 1913 at Maidenhead, Berkshire to Arthur Denison Smith, (born London 1873, died Bournemouth on the 18th September 1939), and Ethel Maud Smith nee Duncan.

They had one son, Anthony Irving Phelps, named after his uncle, born in 1950 at Lambeth, London, who died at Wandsworth, London on the 6th of October 1952; an unhappy coincidence as you will see. There were also 2 daughters recorded on a Public Member's tree on Ancestry but a reference to only one possible daughter born in 1948 has been found.

Peter Horsley Phelps died on the 5th of October 1986, aged 78, at Earlswood, Redhill, Surrey. Monica Denison Phelps died in November 2004 aged 91, at Wandsworth, London.

Anthony Irving Phelps was also educated at Felsted Boarding school, about 1930, where he is listed as having played cricket for the school, again unfortunately with no great success. He went on to Peterhouse, Cambridge, the oldest and smallest of the Cambridge Colleges, where he is remembered on the College War Memorial. No information could be found about his time at Peterhouse or what subjects he chose to follow.

Soon after the outbreak of war he joined the Royal Air Force Volunteer Reserve and the London Gazette for the 5th of September 1941 records he was promoted to L.A.C on the 19th of July 1941.

At some time he had obviously learned to fly because by 1942, 103007 Flying Office Anthony Irving Phelps was posted to 37Sfts (Service Flying School) at McCall Field, Calgary, Alberta, Canada, originally established by the RAF on the 22nd of October 1941.

McCall Field was named in honour of WW1 hero Captain Fred McCall, RAF. Although an RAF base it was run under the administrative and operational control of the RCAF who eventually took it over. It was closed as a training school on the 10th March 1944 and became known as Calgary International Airport in 1966. Coincidentally the grandfather of Kate Middleton, Duchess of Cambridge, Peter Middleton, was also a Flying Instructor with 37Sfts at the same time as Anthony Phelps.

On the 12th of October 1942 Flying Officer Phelps (Flying Instructor) took, 77954 Flight Lt. Robert J. Warner, (pupil pilot) for a training flight in Harvard Mk2 s/n AJ898. At the same time 1125880 LAC H. C. Cromack was flying in Harvard Mk2 s/n AJ854.

At approximately 11.25 hours the aircraft collided at 500 feet and both went straight down and hit the ground 1.5 miles west of the relief landing ground at Airdrie, Alberta. AJ854 was totally destroyed killing LAC Cromack instantly. AJ898 burst into flames and F/O Phelps and F/Lt Warner died in the resulting fire.

They are all three buried at Calgary. Information comes from 'Wings over Alberta', University of Alberta Archives and rafcommands.com.

The Commonwealth War Graves Commission records that Anthony Irving Phelps, son of Dr. J. H. Phelps and Mrs Phelps of Great Malvern was buried at Calgary (Burnsland) Cemetery, Lot 46 Block 8 Section G. in October 1942. He was 31 years old. He is also commemorated on a head stone in St. James' Church Cemetery, West Malvern, Worcestershire which includes Phyllis Margaret Parker (aunt) age 2 days, buried in Old Smethwick cemetery.

John Reginald Phelps, third son of John Henry and Lucy was most likely also educated at Felsted School but a search of the School website did not find any reference to him, although he is recorded with his brothers on the Worcester C.C. Archive.

In 1935/36 he apparently spent 6 months in USA, the family has links there, because on the 22nd of November 1935 he left Liverpool aboard SS Laconia bound for New York. He was aged 22 and described as 'Engineer', giving his last UK address as Millbrook, Albert Road South, Great Malvern. He returned to the UK aboard SS Scythia from New York arriving at Liverpool on the 4th of May 1936, giving the same personal information as before. The probate records for his father give his occupation in 1947 as 'Works Manager'.

John Reginald Phelps married Marjorie Ann Taylor at Trumpington Parish Church, Cambridge on the 28th of October 1939. It is not known if they had any children. John Reginald died in May 1996 at Bedford, aged 83 and his wife Marjorie died in January 1997 at Bedford also aged 83.

During 1935 to 1937 St. Clare was apparently vacant.

Fig. 21 The Burial Plot Of The Phelps Family In St. James' Cemetery In West Malvern

Fig. 22 The Inscription For John Henry Phelps

Fig. 23 The Inscription For Lucy Olive Phelps

2.9 Constance Elizabeth Bairstow nee Hiley (St. Clare 1937 to 1941)

Constance Elizabeth Hiley was the fourth of nine children and second daughter of Rev. Richard William Hiley (born on the 12th of September 1824 at Leeds, Yorkshire, died on the 3rd of November 1912 at Boston Spa, Yorkshire), and his wife Isabella, nee Jessop, (born in Wombwell, Yorkshire on the 28th of April 1832, died on the 14th of December 1909 at Wighill, Wetherby, Yorkshire).

Constance was born on the 28th of June 1865 at Thorp Arch, Yorkshire, where her father was the Principal of Thorp Arch Grange School, one of several schools founded by his father, Richard Hiley. The school had been founded in the 1840's and Rev. Hiley bought it from his father in 1861 when it had 41 male pupils. He became Vicar of Wighill in 1863, taking over from his father in law Thomas Jessop and installing his brother Alfred Hiley as curate. Several other relatives of the Hiley family were also ordained ministers.

As reported by Peter Cole, who has done extensive research on his wife's relatives, Rev. Hiley wrote in the family bible " Our fourth child was born June 28th, 1865 at 9.25 am; christened by me at Wighill Church August 7th, 1865, with names of Constance Elizabeth. Mrs Newenham, Mrs Wilks, and Rev. J. Lawrence, incumbent of St. Michael's, Liverpool were sponsors."

Although Rev. Hiley and two of his daughters are recorded at Grange School on the 2nd of April 1871, Constance and her mother are recorded as boarders at The Green, West Side, Thorp Arch, with Ann Mason, age 66 and her daughter Eleanor age 24. Whether these two were relations with whom they were visiting at the time is not known.

On the 3rd of April 1881 Constance, aged 16 and described as 'Scholar', is recorded living at Grange School with her parents and on the 5th of April 1891, aged 25, she is recorded at St. Mary Bishophill Junior School, Mount Vale, York. The record definitely describes her as 'Scholar' but it is more likely that she was there as a Governess or Teacher since her name is recorded, with other staff members, before those of the pupils, whose ages range from 10 to 15 years.

In 1891 Rev. Richard William Hiley retired from Thorp Arch Grange School and moved to Wighill where he, Isabella and daughter Mabel, aged 19, were recorded living at Wighill Vicarage. He wrote several books about Private Schooling and also Theology and it was while at Wighill in 1899 he published his 'Memories of Half a Century'; his books are freely available on the internet.

On the 31st of March 1901 Constance, aged 35 is recorded with her father at Wighill, presumably at the Vicarage, although this is not clear from the census records, together with her youngest brother Frederick, a student at Queens College, Oxford, who by 1911 was an Assistant Librarian at the British Museum, London.

Her mother Isabella was recorded at 8 West Street, Scarborough visiting with Florence Dawson, age 28, her sisters Laura, Grace and Amy and a brother C. W. They were the children of John Miles Dawson and his wife Elizabeth, formerly of Brook Hall, Wighill. It is not known if they were related.

In 1903 Constance married James Bairstow and her father wrote in the family bible – "April 28. On this day my daughter Constance Elizabeth was married at Wighill Church by her uncle Alfred, (Vicar of Walton), and Rev. Pulleine, Vicar of Sutton-in-Craven, to my former pupil James Bairstow, of Spring Field, Cross Hills, near Keighley. May God bless them."

When Constance married James she became part of a very wealthy and influential family whose history is very closely linked with the development of the area now known as Sutton in Craven, in the West Riding of Yorkshire. At the beginning of the 19th century John Bairstow, a corn miller, grandfather of James, moved his family from Halifax to the village of Sutton, and on the 6th of October 1809 he bought Sutton Mill from David McRobin of Royd House, Haworth. John and his sons Thomas and Matthew carried on the corn milling business at Sutton Mill until 1838.

Traditionally spinning and weaving wool had been carried on domestically in Sutton from the 1500's, but between 1790 and 1810 several small commercial firms, using looms powered by water, were introduced. These were resented by local people as they thought that they were taking work from the hand loom weavers and action against them was taken in 1827 when many looms were broken.

The Bairstow's, however, recognised the potential of the new technology and in 1838 a new mill was built about a quarter of a mile from Sutton. The firm of T. & M. Bairstow was established and became the focus of development of a 'new' village known as Sutton Mill. As the firm progressed a number of extensions were built and the villages of Sutton and Sutton Mill eventually became one. The firm employed over 800 local people, as recorded in the 1851-1871 censuses, and built homes for them to rent around New Mill which, though small, were an improvement on the cramped conditions of the old village, in spite of the fact that water was only available from 't'well' until 1860.

In addition to the homes for workers a number of larger properties, standing in their own grounds, were built by individual owners including Royd Hill, which became the home of Thomas Bairstow from 1840 until his death in 1867, Knott House and Springfield, the homes of Matthew Bairstow until his death in 1881. Springfield then became the home of James and it was there that he and Constance spent the whole of their married life. An excellent, up to date website and forum by Paul Wilkinson, is the source for much of this information and has much more to offer.

James Bairstow was born on the 4th of February 1852 at the Knott, Eastburn. He was the third child of six, the only son, born to Matthew Bairstow, (born about 1816 in Steeton in Eastburn, died on the 7th of July 1881 at Springfield), and Susannah Hooson, (born about 1816 in Northowram, died on the 21st of May 1888 at Springfield).

No record has so far been found for the 1861 census, but on the 2nd of April 1871 James is recorded with his parents, and three servants, at Springfield and, although no occupation is given, it is believed that he was already involved in the family firm. As quoted earlier, it is known that he had received his education from Constance's father, Richard Hiley, but no dates are given and he was not recorded as a pupil at Thorp Arch School in 1861.

Although four sons were born to Thomas Bairstow and his wife Elizabeth Ingilby, three of them had died by 1861 and the fourth, Walter Bairstow, does not appear to have had any interest in following his father into T. & M. Bairstow Ltd, being recorded as 'Gentleman' or 'living off Bank Dividends'. Thus, James was the only second generation Bairstow recorded with the firm in 1881; however, his aunt Sarah, having married George Spencer, an Attorney at Law, also had four sons and one of them, John Bairstow Spencer (born 30th of August 1836) had become the first non-Bairstow member of the management, joining the firm as a junior partner in 1869 following the death of Thomas.

On the 3rd of April 1881 John is recorded living at Knott House the original home of Matthew Bairstow and his family and by the 5th of April 1891 he was living at Royd Hill, the former home of Thomas and his family, which he then passed on to his son Thomas when he died in 1900. In 1903 Thomas jnr. bought some land and built a new house, Lyndhurst, where he lived until 1920 when he sold it to Charles Malcolm Bateman for £6,000 (£252,000 at 2012 values).

By a strange coincidence, Walter Bairstow was recorded in 1901 living at Kenilworth House, Kenilworth Road, Lillington, Warwickshire which, in 1891, had been the home of Charles James Shaw, brother of Helen Elizabeth Makin nee Shaw, the main beneficiary of the estate of Edward Ratheram, the first owner of St. Clare.

From 1881 onwards, following the death of his father, James Bairstow is recorded as a Worsted Spinner and Manufacturer, head of the firm T. & M. Bairstow Ltd; in both 1891 and 1901 three servants are listed at Springfield. James was 51 when he married Constance Elizabeth Hiley, aged 37, in 1903 and she moved 28 miles from Wighill to Springfield, Steeton in Eastburn.

Little is known of the life of Constance and James after they married. On the 2nd of April 1911 James is recorded as 'married' but no census record for Constance has been found. Springfield was recorded as having 13 rooms and there were 4 servants, including a Mary Garside, aged 33, who was employed as Cook.

The Bairstow family had been responsible for a number of developments in Sutton over the years; for instance, there had been no church in Sutton until Thomas died in 1867 leaving money for a building, still in use today, which was built in 1869 and dedicated to St. Thomas on St. Thomas' day.

They were also responsible for building an institute, including a billiard room and a swimming bath, for the use of local people. They appear to have been well regarded in the area; the National School logbook, recorded on the Sutton Village website, lists visits from various family members to 'hear the children sing'; events held at Royd Hill for the school children; and on the occasion of the marriage of James's cousin Ellen Bairstow to Joshua Robert Jennings in 1881 the school was closed for the day.

Sadly there are no references whatsoever to the marriage of James and Constance and no record was found of her presence at Springfield, although James is mentioned in the school log book several times in his capacity as head of T. & M. Bairstow Ltd.

There was another mill producing worsted in Sutton, in addition to Sutton Mill, which was known as Hartley's or Greenroyd Mill, and on the 3rd of November 1911 James bought it from J. W. Hartley so it became a branch of T. & M. Bairstow Ltd. When he died in 1912 J. W. Hartley left land to be made into a park, and, in the tradition of the Bairstow family, James added to this amenity; it eventually included tennis courts, paddling pool and gardens.

There were no children born to James and Constance to follow him into T. & M Bairstow. Ltd, so around 1911 two of James's nephews joined the family firm; Charles Malcolm Bateman, youngest son of Ann Elizabeth Bairstow and William Frederick Bateman, whose family were involved in preparing cards for Jacquard looms, and Norman Bairstow Chaffers, eldest son of Mary Maria Bairstow and Dr. Edward Chaffers, a local GP and Surgeon. They were known to employees and villagers alike as Colonel Bateman and Colonel Chaffers, following their service in Duke of Wellington's West Riding Regiment in WW1 and subsequent involvement with the Territorials.

James and Constance continued to live at Springfield until 1930 when James died on the 31st of May at 77 Clarendon Road, Leeds leaving an estate valued at £424,007 8s 3d (£21,528,385 at 2012 values).

Peter Cole writes that the Keighley News for the 7th of June 1930 had many glowing tributes to James, but he felt that although he was 'clearly an exceptional man' he was also a 'bit of a loner' and had the impression he had 'not integrated well with the rest of Connie's family'. James made good provision for his wife after his death, ensuring that she could live comfortably, and then left the 'bulk of his fortune to the Church and other charities'.

T. & M. Bairstow continued under Colonels Bateman and Chaffers during their lifetimes, and then under the direction of 'Mr Malcolm' the son of Colonel Bateman; the firm celebrated its Centenary in 1938 and it finally ceased trading around 1970.

In 1996 Bairstow's Mill was demolished; only the flagpole remains, being re-sited in Crag Nook Delph by the Sutton Conservation Society. Greenroyd Mill has recently been redeveloped into apartments available for rent by local residents with incomes of less that £30,000 per annum.

Following James' death in 1930, Connie left Yorkshire at the age of 65 and seems to have eventually lost contact with her family of nephews and nieces on the Hiley side, but Peter Cole reports that she had always been very generous to her relatives, paying for the education of at least two, possibly four, of her grandnieces including his wife. He also says that following James' death 'she moved around a lot, living in hotels'; no mention of her is made on the Sutton in Craven Village website and a request entered on the forum for any information or memories anyone may have of her has received no responses.

However, Tony Cole has very kindly sent a copy of an extract from a letter written in 1992 by Dorothy Kirkby, a daughter of Connie's sister Mabel; she was then aged 91. This gives the only insights we have into life at Springfield. In it she suggests that after James' death Connie moved to a nursing home in Wales where she presumed that she died; we now know that this was not the case.

Dorothy also describes childhood visits to Springfield – "a beautiful house with big drawing room, dining room, study and basement dairy" where there were pans of milk and cream that came from James' own cattle, "little longhorns kept in the hills". He also had his own stables which Dorothy visited "after church on Sundays to give the horses sugar nobs". She comments on the beautiful meals prepared by Mary, "a wonderful cook", particularly recalling the trifles that she made using the home produced cream.

She refers to the fact that Connie had no children, suggesting that this was something that was very much regretted, which would bear out the comments concerning Connie's generosity to her family.

Dorothy recalls that James used a dog cart to get around the estate "with a man behind in cocked hat and uniform", whilst Connie had a "Victoria" pulled by two horses named Romulus and Remus, driven by "Taylor the coachman in full rig"; he lived over the stables. This was later replaced by motor cars driven by Bismark Heaton, Connie's chauffeur. In 1911 he was recorded with his family living at Knott House; he appears to have died in Yorkshire in 1956 aged 86.

Constance Elizabeth Bairstow is recorded in the telephone directory as living at Shelton Hall, Shrewsbury from 1931-1935 and on the 15th of October 1936 she is recorded on the Electoral Register living at The County Hotel, Abbey Road, Great Malvern. The County Hotel was probably the most expensive hotel in Malvern at that time; originally built as the Hydropathic Establishment of Dr. James Wilson, it is currently Park View Apartments, 33 Abbey Road.

On the 15th of October 1937, and subsequently in 1938 and 1939, she is listed as living at St. Clare, Priory Road, Great Malvern; 'S J' is entered after name, believed to mean 'Special Juror'. Listed with her at St. Clare are Dorothy May Farley, Emma Florence Perkins and Mary Garside, believed to be the same person recorded as Cook at

Springfield in 1911 and referred to by Dorothy Kirkby in her letter; it looks as though she brought her servants with her.

There were no Electoral registers kept after 1939 for the duration of WW2, but Connie is recorded in the telephone directory at St. Clare (Tel. No. Malvern 330), until 1941. Where she went after this was not clear, but Peter reports the following entry in the family Bible:

"1947: On May 2nd died Constance Elizabeth, daughter of Rev. R. W. Hiley and widow of James Bairstow, aged 81. Buried on May 6th in Llanrhydd Churchyard, near Ruthin, N. Wales."

The only death certificate reference found for Constance Elizabeth Bairstow was North East Cheshire 10a 380 Apr-Jun 1947. This is not the registration district for Ruthin; the death certificate revealed that she had died at Cheadle Royal Hospital, Cheadle, Cheshire on the date as recorded in the family bible. The cause of death was given as pneumonia and senile decay and the informant was 'M. C. Hood, Acting Medical Superintendent of Cheadle Royal'; this suggests no members of the family were present at the time.

Cheadle Royal Hospital was previously known as Manchester Royal Lunatic Asylum and is still a Psychiatric Hospital. It is situated between Heald Green and Cheadle on the Wilmslow Road. Built in 1848-1849 in the Elizabethan Style, it is considered to be an important example of the Victorian asylum system.

How or why Connie came to be in a hospital in Cheshire is not known. Cheadle Royal is about 60 miles away from Ruthin where the family records say Connie is buried, and they did not know the reason why she is buried there.

The address given for Connie on the death certificate was 'Pembridge' Graham Road, Malvern, Worcestershire which suggests that when she left St. Clare she had stayed in the town.

'Pembridge' is currently run as a Bed and Breakfast business and an enquiry was made of the current owners to see if they had any records back to 1947 which would show whether it had been a hotel or private house. Although they did not have complete records they were able to confirm that it had been a hotel in the 1930's and a B&B or hotel in the 1950's and 1960's, so in view of Peter's comments that Connie had 'lived in hotels', it would seem most likely that it was a hotel when she lived there.

The London Gazette dated the 23rd of May 1947 has a request for anyone with a claim on her estate giving the address at the time of death as 'c/o Provincial Bank, Malvern' with former addresses of Springfield, Keighley and St. Clare, Malvern; this again would suggest that she was living in hotels in the Malvern area after leaving St. Clare.

The executors named in the London Gazette were Connie's brother Frederick Charles William Hiley and James' nephew Alfred Bairstow Clarkson. The solicitors named as 'Spencer Clarkson Limited of 40 North Street, Keighley' were also relatives from the Bairstow side.

A copy of probate records together with a copy of Connie's will has been obtained from the Probate Office in Leeds. The will was written on the 8th of September 1942 with the address given as c/o Provincial Bank as previously recorded. Further indication she was no longer living at St. Clare and was probably staying in a hotel at that time.

The first request was to be buried in Llanrhydd Churchyard, near Ruthin, but no reason for this request was given. The very detailed will bequeathed all personal and household items to her surviving siblings for them to distribute, with the exception of a diamond pendant given to her by James on their wedding day, which was to be sold for the benefit of his nieces.

After several specific legacies, including one to Bismark Heaton, described as her Chauffeur, and payment of any fees, the residue was to be invested with the interest generated to benefit Connie's sister Mabel, passing to her children on her death.

The Will was witnessed by R. Ernestwood and G. Rodney Winter, Dental Surgeons of 12 Princes Square, Harrogate, Yorkshire and probate was granted to the executors at Wakefield on the 15th of July 1947 for a net estate of £17,623 12s 3d (£599,202 at 2012 values).

Photographs of Constance Elizabeth have kindly been provided by Tony Cole.

Fig. 24 Constance Elizabeth Bairstow nee Hiley

Fig. 25 An older Constance Elizabeth Bairstow nee Hiley

2.10 Admiralty WRNS Hostel (St. Clare, 1941 to 1945)

From 1941 to 1945 St. Clare may have been used as a hostel for Members of the Women's Royal Naval Service (WRNS) based at HMS Duke located on the TRE / RRE / RSRE / DRA / DERA / QinetiQ site, St. Andrews Road.

HMS Duke was a navy training establishment between 1941 and 1946 before becoming the Royal Radar Establishment (RRE).

Details are held in the National Archives and also in the Worcester Council Records office of a proposed hot water scheme installed by W. James, builders of Malvern., ref. 705:876/BA8077/53/ii, 1943-44, about 50 letters, specifications and invoices.

The Planning Application was Admiralty Contract W.77, 1943 - 44, Admiralty Offices, 243 Hagley Road, Birmingham 16.

The Application was for the addition of a further hot water storage vessel, a new gas boiler, and a number of new pipes and outlets. Extensive repair work was also carried out on the windows. The cost in 1944 was £359 17s 5d, which at 2012 value is £13,315

Attempts to find out more about this period through the National Archives have so far proved fruitless and a request for anyone with any knowledge of WRNS at Malvern placed on an internet forum has had no response.

Malvern was chosen at the beginning of hostilities as a suitable 'refuge for government departments' and in 'The History of Malvern College' it is recorded that the College was evacuated to Blenheim Palace so that the College building could be prepared as 'wartime quarters for the Admiralty under its First Lord, Winston Churchill'.

In the event it was never used for this purpose and the boys returned, only to be evacuated to Harrow in 1942 when the '1942 Government Restriction (Malvern) Order' came into force and the College was used to house T.R.E. from Christchurch, Hampshire. Malvern became a closed area with compulsory billeting being arranged and hotels commandeered for use. It is likely that St. Clare was annexed by the Admiralty at this time and prepared for use but never actually occupied.

Records, held by Worcestershire Archives and Archaeology Service at The Hive, Worcester, show that St. Ronan's was requisitioned by the Admiralty in 1942, but it's subsequent use during WW2 is not known. It was however taken over by the Women's Land Army in 1947 for use as a Hostel; it is not recorded how long it was used for this purpose.

This agrees with information from Carol Hutber, in conversation, when she recalled being visited by someone who had lived in the property at that time and they were able to point out how the rooms had been used.

The Electoral Register for Bewdley (Great Malvern) has no entries for 1945, 1946 and 1947 and it is assumed that St. Clare was vacant. The Register was recorded on the 15th of October each year.

2.11 Griffith Rowland Owen, Laura Margaret Owen, formerly Evans, nee Jones (St. David's Hotel 1948)

Griffith Rowland Owen was born on the 21st of February 1904 at Bronaber, Bontddu, Dolgelly, Merioneth. He was the eldest child of John Owen (born at Bontddu about 1868) who was a carpenter at the local Gold Mine and Ann Catherine Richards (born 1874 at Dolgelly). He had a sister Jennie who was born in 1906. His father had been married before and in the 1911 census a stepsister Margaret was recorded with the family at Bronaber, Bontddu.

On the 19th of October 1925, when he was 21 years old, Griffith Rowland Owen was married by license to a widow, Laura Margaret Evans, age recorded on the certificate as 30, at Aberayron, Cardiganshire; this would give her birth date as 1895.

His occupation at that time was given as Motor Mechanic and his address was given as Carno House, Aberayron. Laura Margaret's occupation was not recorded but her address was given as Bondaron, Bontddu. Her father's name was recorded as Evan Rowland Jones (deceased), described as 'Gentleman of Independent' means.

In the census dated the 31st of March 1901 the only Evan Rowland Jones with a daughter Laura Margaret of suitable age was recorded at 18 Sandstone Road, West Derby, Liverpool, Lancashire, working as a market gardener, and her birth date was given as 1892 with the birthplace United States of America. No birth certificate could be located for a Laura Margaret Jones in the UK for either 1892 or 1895 but a marriage reference was found for a possible marriage to Arthur Goronwy Evans at Tranmere, Birkenhead, Cheshire in 1910.

On the 2nd of April 1911 the couple were recorded at 181 Wrotham Road, Gravesend, Kent together with a daughter Mary Kathleen Evans born in 1910. Arthur's occupation was recorded as school master. The birthdate and place for Laura Margaret confirmed the information given in the 1901 census showing that she was born in Brooklyn, New York, USA.

It was however, not certain that Elizabeth Jones nee Roberts, recorded as wife of Evan Rowland Jones in 1901, was the mother of Laura Margaret. Elizabeth was born in 1875 in Liverpool and had married Evan Rowland there in 1898, giving birth to a daughter Ann in 1899. No record was found for the couple in 1911 and it is possible that Elizabeth Jones died in Liverpool in 1901 aged 26. No record has been identified for Evan Rowland Jones.

Arthur Goronwy Evans enlisted in the 11th Battalion of the Royal Welsh Fusiliers on the 8th of December 1915 and his military service records gave his birth date as 1881 and the date of marriage to Laura Margaret as the 9th of August 1910 at Tranmere, Cheshire. The birth of Mary Kathleen was recorded as the 25th of December 1910 at Gravesend and there was second child recorded – Arthur Goronwy Evans born 18th of April 1913 at Greenhithe, Kent. The address given for Laura Margaret, as his next of kin, was Storridge School, Malvern, Worcestershire.

From census records for the 3rd of April 1881 it was found that Arthur Goronwy was living with his parents and older brother Llewellyn Lloyd Evans at Deunant School, Aberdaron, Pwllheli. His father, Abraham Llewellyn Evans, was an Elementary Schoolmaster, and his mother was Mary Catherine Lloyd.

On the 5th of April 1891 the family, now with 3 more children, were living at Tan Lan, Maentwrog, Caernarvonshire where Abraham was teaching and in 1901 he was at Storridge School Malvern, living at Storridge Road, Cradley, Bromyard. In 1901 Arthur Goronwy was an assistant school master at Portishead, Somerset where he is recorded as a boarder at 5 Pier Road, Royal Terrace, Portishead.

By the 2nd of April 1911 Abraham Evans was recorded as Headmaster of Storridge School and it would appear, therefore, that Laura Margaret and her two children were living with her in laws in 1915 while Arthur was serving in the Army.

On the 28th of October 1916 Arthur Goronwy Evans was killed in action in Serbia and was buried in the Karasouli Military Cemetery, Polikastro, Thessalonica. The grave reference recorded on the Commonwealth War Graves Commission 'Debt of Honour' was C 532.

Following her marriage to Griffith Rowland Owen, the couple were living at the Bridgend Temperance Hotel, Aberayron and on the 28th February 1928 Laura Margaret, as keeper of the Temperance hotel, was served with a petition of bankruptcy.

A summary administration order was issued at Aberystwyth Court on the 24th of March 1928. This was followed by a meeting on the 13th of April and a public hearing on the 19th of April, also at Aberystwyth as recorded in the London Gazette.

Application for discharge from the Bankruptcy was not made until the 19th of February 1943 in the Town Hall at Aberystwyth. A further hearing was held on 22nd of October and the application for discharge was refused on the grounds of proof of facts required.

The last day for receipt of proof of facts was set for the 13th of February 1946 but on the 21st of December 1945 the discharge was granted on the payment of £150 (£5,250 at 2012 values).

In 1944 Mary Kathleen Evans married Ronald Henry Mildred at Edmonton, Middlesex. It is possible that a son was born in Norwich, Norfolk in 1945 who is still alive today.

In October 1948, Laura Margaret and Griffith Rowland Owen are recorded in the Electoral Register living at 34 Priory Road, Malvern; it is most likely that they purchased the building from the Admiralty after the end of the War.

Anne Noble confirms that they were running the property as St. David's Hotel; she has a copy of their brochure from her grandparents, William and Esme Noble, who purchased the hotel from 'a Welshman' in 1950. It is suggested that the business was in a rundown state when they acquired it.

John Noble recalls meeting Griffith Owen, but not Laura, when he accompanied his father to view the property prior to purchase and he was uncertain as to the exact nature of the business at that time. He thought it was being run as a Care Home and commented that all the occupants were required to attend 'Prayers' before breakfast every morning.

No further records were found for Griffith Rowland Owen and no death reference has been identified in that name in the UK, but he apparently died before 1976 because Laura is described as 'widow of Griffith Rowland Owen' on her death certificate.

Her last permanent address was recorded as Long Cottage, Wrington, Somerset but she died in Mowbray Nursing Home, Victoria Road, Malvern, Worcestershire on the 17th of July 1976 at the age of 86. The date of birth recorded on the death certificate was the 7th of October 1889 in the USA. If this is correct, then her age at the time of her marriage to Griffith Rowland Owen was 36 and not 30 as stated on the marriage certificate.

The cause of death was given as pneumonia, congestive heart failure and generalised arteriosclerosis, as certified by Adrian L McKracken M.B. Her death was registered by her son in law Ronald Henry Mildred of Long Cottage, Wrington. Following cremation her ashes were buried at Malvern Cemetery, Madresfield Road, Malvern in CP (cremation plot) D 12 on the 23rd of July 1976; the plot is unmarked but lies to the right of that for Reg Lower

The Electoral Register for Bewdley (Great Malvern) has no entries for 1949 and 1950 and it is assumed that St. Clare was vacant.

From this point on personal details will be limited to persons known to have died, unless specific permission has been given, since it is not good practise to include personal details of living persons; full information will however be held in unpublished records.

2.12 William Noble and Esme Noble (nee Willetts) (The Clans Hotel, 1950 to 1964)

William Noble was born at 35 School Street, Fraserburgh, Aberdeenshire, Scotland on the 4th of October 1892, one of thirteen children born to Andrew Noble (born Fraserburgh about 1859,) and Margaret Trail (born Fraserburgh on the 12th of January 1862, died on the 14th of February 1931).

Fraserburgh was one of the main ports for the herring fishing industry and many of the people of the town, both men and women, made their living from catching and curing herring. William's grandfather, Alexander Noble, was a fisherman living in Shore Street, quite close to the harbour, as were several other family members, but his father Andrew and Uncle William worked as coopers making barrels for transporting cured herring as far afield as Russia and the Baltic States.

The fishermen went out at night and on arrival back in port the following morning the 'gutting quines', as the women were known, were employed to gut and salt the fish and pack them into barrels which were then sealed by the 'coopers loons'. The herring fishing season began in the Hebrides in the springtime and by Midsummer the shoals had reached Fraserburgh, eventually progressing as far south as East Anglia by the end of the season.

It was customary for the 'gutting quines' and 'coopers loons' to follow the progress of the herring shoals throughout the season, living in small huts or lodging houses in the different areas; this continued into the 1920's and may well have been the lifestyle followed by earlier generations of Nobles, although there is no indication in the records that this was the lifestyle of Andrew and his family.

There was a common saying that ' Cod and corn dinna gaun the gither', implying that fishing families and farming families tended not to intermarry, but this did not apply to William's parents. Whilst Andrew came from a fishing family, Margaret Trail was a farmer's daughter from Mosside, Fraserburgh; their children do not appear to have followed either tradition, although two daughters did work in the 'Meat and Fish Factory' in their teens.

The boys would have been of an age to have served in WW1; there is a record of the death of an Andrew Noble born on the 23rd of June 1889 at Fraserburgh, who was lost at sea in 1917 aboard HMS Deliverer, but nothing conclusive has been found which would link him to the family and there are a large number of Noble's in Fraserburgh! No other military records have been found with names appropriate to the family.

Andrew and Margaret had married on the 5th of June 1884 and lived at 35 School Street, Fraserburgh, near the centre of the town. In the 1901 census dated the 31st of March they and their children, including William who was a 'scholar', were recorded living at 1 Dickson's Building, Caroline Place, which was just round the corner from School Street. No further census record for the family has been seen.

In conversation Anne Noble nee Burcher, granddaughter of William and Esme, reported that she did not know exactly when William left Scotland but he was unable to serve in WW1 due to a damaged heart and during that time he was attached to the Ministry of Food where he was involved in assessing the quality of the food provided for the troops.

He eventually moved into the Midlands, where on the 22nd of July 1919 he married Esme Maud Willetts at the Parish Church, Sutton Coldfield, Warwickshire. Esme was aged 22, William 26, and he was recorded on the marriage certificate as working as a 'Clerk'. His father Andrew Noble was recorded as a 'Cooper'; Esme's father was given as Reuben Willetts, 'Caterer'.

Esme Maude Willetts was born on the 11th of January 1897 at the 'Horn and Trumpet' a Public House.in Bewdley; her granddaughter suggests this was something of which she was not proud, preferring to call it 'a Hotel'.

She was the eldest child of three, two girls and a boy, born to Reuben William Willetts, (born at Walmsley, in 1873, died on the 11th of January 1939 in Sutton Coldfield), and Alice Annie Willetts nee Willetts, (born in 1871 at Sutton Coldfield, died in 1996 at Sutton Coldfield); they were paternal first cousins, their fathers being brothers Reuben and Thomas Willetts, sons of John Willetts and Hannah Yates.

On the 5th of April 1891 Reuben William was single and recorded as a Grocer's Assistant living and working at 128 Broad Street Birmingham, but by the 31st of March 1901 he was married and recorded as a Commercial Traveller. The family were then living with Alice's widowed mother Martha at Ashcroft Lane, Shenstone, Staffordshire. Reuben William and Alice had married at Lichfield, Staffordshire in January 1896.

Both Reuben William and Alice Annie had been brought up in the licensed trade, a connection which went back to their grandfather, John Willetts, who had combined working as a forgeman with running several public houses in Sutton Coldfield, Warwickshire, including 'The Gate' and 'The Dog Inn'. Reuben's father also worked as a forgeman and grocer and ran 'The Hawthorn Bush' at Sutton Coldfield and 'The Swan Inn' at Washwood Heath, Birmingham, whilst Alice's father was a blacksmith and publican with public houses including, 'The Trooper' at Wall nr Lichfield and 'The Station Hotel' at Rugeley, both in Staffordshire.

It was not, therefore, very surprising to find Reuben William and Alice Annie recorded on the 2nd of April 1911 as Licensees of 'The White Horse', Whitehouse Road, Sutton Coldfield, together with Esme, her sister Evelyn Mabel and brother Thomas Dudley, all at school at that time.

During WW1 Esme, who had previously had no occupation, decided to 'do her bit for the war effort' by volunteering to drive taxis for a relative, thought to be Walter Willetts. Anne suggested that her grandmother was not the best organised lady and when driving a soldier to the station she attempted to drive between two trams, causing the soldier to climb out of the taxi via the roof. He felt he would be 'safer on the bus'. Her driving career ended when she checked the petrol tank, located beneath the passenger seat, using a lighted match!

Later, Reuben and his family moved to 'Beccles', Whitehouse Common Road, Sutton Coldfield, Warwickshire, a large house, now demolished, which he had built two doors away from the Whitehorse Public House. Anne said that her great grandfather who 'lived life to the full' had probably made, and lost, £2,000,000 during his lifetime!

John Noble's recollections of his grandfather were of a man rather larger than life, who had a lavish lifestyle and for whom 'only the best of everything' was good enough. He had a number of business interests in addition to the Public House and owned several residential properties in the area.

Anne could not say exactly where William and Esme lived following their marriage but it is believed that they lived in a flat above one of the Public Houses run by Reuben Willetts at Reddicap Hill, Sutton Coldfield. At this time William was working for a firm called 'Priory Teas', first as a clerk, as recorded on his marriage certificate, and later as a travelling salesman.

On the 29th of April 1920 their first child Margaret Noble was born, the birth was registered at Aston, Warwickshire the registration district for Sutton Coldfield at that time. They moved to Tynemouth when Margaret, Anne's mother, was about two years old and they lived there for about ten years.

Their second child, a son, was born in 1924 in Tynemouth, Northumberland; Angela Martell, a distant relative of Esme, reported that her grandmother, Annie Rose Newey, who was a first cousin-once-removed of Esme, was living in that area with her husband Alexander Sangster. Annie Rose apparently went there originally as a barmaid and Angela wondered if William and Esme were visiting them at the time their son was born; apparently this was not the case.

In 1926 their second daughter, Audrey Evelyn Noble, was born in Sutton Coldfield, Warwickshire on the 4th of February that year. Anne said that she had talked about this with her uncle but he did not know why Audrey was born there as the family home was still in Tynemouth.

During the long school holiday in August the children always went to Fraserburgh. Their luggage was sent ahead of them in a trunk that William had specially made for the purpose. Anne still has this trunk which is now used to hold all her treasured items of family memorabilia.

When they left Tynemouth they lived briefly at 'Beccles', Whitehouse Common Road, Sutton Coldfield, eventually moving to 156 Station Road, Boldmere, Sutton Coldfield where they lived throughout the War years.

Reuben Willetts was Managing Director of a Flour Mill in Sutton Coldfield, one of a number of Mills owned by the company originally founded by John Drew in the Birmingham area as early as 1857. William was employed there in a senior position for several years before he bought the Clans Hotel. Anne believes that the Mill run successfully by William was situated in Wellington Road, Perry Barr, Sutton Coldfield.

A Birmingham University Archaeological Report, Project No. 1398 dated 2006, for a site close to the present Crown and Cushion Public House, Wellington Road, Perry Barr, includes information about a Mill, named Perry Mill, situated on the banks of the River Tame. It was one of four included in the Domesday Book and was known to have been used as a corn mill in the sixteenth and seventeenth centuries, then briefly as a rolling mill before being returned to a corn mill by 1818; the Mill buildings were finally demolished in 1980, a model farm being built on the site.

An entry in Bennetts Business Directory for Warwickshire 1914 records the following - 'J. Drew & Sons Ltd, Perry Barr Mills, est. 1858, millers and corn merchants, self-raising flour manufacturers'. This was said to be 'near the Crown and Cushion Public House'. Although there is no direct proof it is likely that this was the Mill run by William until the late 1940's.

During WW2 Anne said that her mother Margaret had served in the ATS; when she was demobilised she too worked at the Flour Mill with her father, acting as secretary, and when the business was sold to Absolom, Crocker & Co, Tea Merchants from London William retired, while Margaret remained at the Mill.

John Noble said while deciding what direction his future should take his father had advice from a friend named Doble, who was an Estate Agent in Birmingham. He recalled with some amusement the difference in heights of the two men, William being fairly short while Mr Doble was very tall. He suggested that when they were travelling round to look at properties they could have been mistaken for a comedy double act since they often signed into hotels as 'Noble & Doble'.

William originally agreed to purchase a hotel in Teignmouth, South Devon, but, as often happened at that time he was 'gazumped' by someone who made a better offer. He then had the choice of running a farm in Devon or a hotel in Malvern.

In 1950 John accompanied 'Noble and Doble' on their visit to St. David's Hotel, 34 Priory Road and he remembers a careful assessment being made of 'how long hot water took to reach the highest bedroom'! It was obviously satisfactory as William bought St. David's Hotel; as a staunch Scot he was however unwilling to continue with that name.

His son had spent some time in Canada and recalled visiting an eating establishment there with a marked Scottish theme named 'The Clans' and, being aware of his father's roots, he suggested this as a possible name for the hotel. Hence the name of the property changed once again and it was known as The Clans Private Hotel until William and Esme left the business.

It seems likely that Esme's experience of living in licensed premises would give her an interest in such work which she could put to good use. In 1950 they were recorded in the telephone directory, and on Electoral Registers, at The Clans Hotel, 34, Priory Road, Malvern, telephone number Malvern 1717.

There were a number of permanent residents at the hotel and during the time they were at The Clans William and Esme did a lot of business with Malvern College parents, particularly at Speech day and ends of terms, becoming good friends with a number of them. Anne particularly remembers the people who developed the children's toy 'Fuzzy Felt' whose son was a boarder at the College. Apparently she received a number of gifts of their products during that time.

Anne remembers her grandmother as 'a great character' who 'liked to entertain with a flourish', but she was a terrible cook, so it was William who undertook all the catering at The Clans whilst Esme dealt with booking and all the 'front of house' arrangements. The modern appliances of fridge and freezer were not available in those days and William would go out each morning to purchase the food for the day. He would always buy whatever each resident fancied - fish for one, meat for another - and prepare everything fresh each day. He had the help of Mrs Baldwin who came in to do the 'rough work', cleaning and changing of beds.

Both Anne and John recalled that Esme was friendly with a lady who ran a hotel a few properties away in Priory Road and that they had an agreement that if one of them were fully booked then they would recommend the other. They believed her name was 'Comont' but could not remember her first name. It is suggested that this would have been Annie Millicent Comont who was running The Sherington Hotel in the early 1950's. More will be said about her later as she subsequently became the owner of The Clans, changing the name yet again to Hotel St. Clare.

William also had an arrangement for mutual advantage with another hotel owner as he was friends with a gentleman who was running Sydney House, Worcester Road at that time. Cooperation between the different businesses helped keep all their hotels profitable.

Esme was particularly fond of the garden, spending as much time in it as possible. She planted many shrubs, including rhododendrons along the front of the property. These were removed when the house was demolished and the front wall, which Anne remembers was already bulging in the 1950's, was entirely rebuilt during the erection of Priory Gardens. Esme grew many of the flowers that were used for decoration in the hotel and cared for all the borders but she employed a man to help with lawn mowing; unfortunately the first one dropped dead one day in the middle of the lawn!

They continued to run The Clans until 1964 and during that time Anne remembers that all her family holidays, particularly Christmas, were spent at the Hotel. Audrey was always listed with her parents on the Electoral Register; she never married but she worked as a telephonist, first for the G.P.O and then for T.R.E.

When William and Esme decided to leave the Clans they needed a house large enough for them to take one of their permanent residents with them. Anne remembers Gladys M. Edwardson, she called her 'Miss Edwardson', as 'a lovely lady' and she went to live with William and Esme in their new home at 14 Carlton Road, Malvern, Worcestershire.

Gladys Edwardson later moved to Andover to live with her niece; her death was recorded at Andover in December 1990 at the age of 96. William and Esme 'downsized' and bought a bungalow which was better suited to their needs at the time, 33 Green Lane, Malvern Wells, Worcestershire.

John Noble was surprised that there was doubt as to whether the property continued to be run as a hotel after his parents sold it. He said that they believed the person who bought it had every intention of continuing the business, even discussing the possibility of fitting it out with tartan curtains and carpets. Unfortunately he could not recall the name of the purchaser and he did not recognise any of the names recorded on the Electoral Roll for the following year.

Just 4 days before leaving The Clans William had suffered his first stroke. He died on the 5th of September 1967 at the Royal Infirmary Ronkswood, Worcester, the cause of death being given as a 'Stokes Adams attack associated with arterio-sclerosis which had caused right sided hemiplegia'; this would mean that he was partially paralysed. The term 'Stokes Adams attack' is rarely used today; it describes a sudden loss of consciousness which may be connected to several different problems including those associated with heart function.

The death was registered by his eldest daughter Margaret Burcher nee Noble of 39 Green Lane Malvern Wells. William Noble was buried at Malvern Wells Cemetery, Green Lane, Malvern Wells in plot Ref. 1157.

Telephone directory entries in the name of E. M. Noble for 1967-1982 suggest that Esme, and presumably Audrey, continued to live at the same house, 33 Green Lane, Malvern Wells, more or less opposite the Malvern Wells Cemetery, until at least 1982 and this has been confirmed by a past neighbour and her granddaughter. Anne reported that Esme lived there until 1985 when she moved to her last permanent address at 2 Hill View Close, Malvern Link where she was nearer to her granddaughter's home.

Esme moved to Malvernbury Nursing Home, Abbey Road, Malvern just 2 days before she died there on the 7th of November 1993 at the age of 96. The cause of death, certified by B. A. Ward M.B, was given as Myocardial Failure and her death was registered by her son, on the 8th of November 1993.

The following week, on the 16th of November, she was buried at Malvern Wells Cemetery, Green Lane, Malvern Wells in the same plot No 1157 as William.

Audrey died 10 years later in March 2003 at the age of 77; her death was registered in Worcester and she too was buried in plot No 1157 at Malvern Wells Cemetery, Green Lane Malvern Wells.

When her parents and sister moved to Malvern, Margaret had remained at 'Beccles' Sutton Coldfield, still working as secretary at the flour mill where she was to hand over to 'the new man' who had been put in as manager by the new owners. His name was William

George Burcher and, according to Anne, they 'hated one another at first'.

However things were to change and in 1952 Margaret and William were married at Malvern; their daughter was born at Sutton Coldfield the following year. They lived at 30 Shipton Road, Sutton Coldfield, Warwickshire, a house that William had bought and lived in himself, during their engagement.

The address given for Margaret on her father's death certificate was 39 Green Lane, Malvern Wells and Anne reported that her parents had bought the bungalow in 1965; she and her mother moved in immediately but William Burcher remained in Sutton Coldfield in order to dispose of his business before retiring to Malvern.

Unfortunately he was taken ill with pneumonia and spent months in hospital during which time Margaret ran the business. A competitor attempted to buy them out, but William refused to sell and for three years Anne said the family lived 'between the shop and the bungalow' until her father died at Sutton Coldfield just before her birthday in 1968.

From then on Margaret Burcher nee Noble is recorded at 39 Green Lane, Malvern Wells, until she moved on her 65th birthday in 1985 to a new, but smaller, house in Sunrise, off Pickersleigh Road, Malvern. She sold that house in 1989 and moved in with her daughter Anne in Albion Road where she lived until she died in October 2001; her death was registered in Malvern.

Both William George and Margaret Burcher are buried in Malvern Wells Cemetery, just two plots away from Esme, William and Audrey.

In August 1954, William and Esme's son had married at the Malvern Register Office. Both bride and groom gave their address as The Clans Hotel but they did not appear on the Electoral Register. They went to live in Cheltenham, where their daughter was born and later moved for a time to Northern Ireland, where he was working as an electrical engineer, before returning to live in Sutton Coldfield. Later they moved to Droitwich and then back to Malvern Link as recorded on Esme's death certificate in November 1993.

He is still alive and well, aged 88 (May 2012) and has lived since 1998 in Devon, as does his daughter, now married. Much of the personal information about the family has been provided by Anne and her Uncle.

The following photographs were kindly provided by Ann Noble and her Uncle.

Fig. 26 William Noble

Fig. 27 Esme Noble, In The Garden Of The Clans Hotel

Fig. 28 Margaret Burcher nee Noble & Audrey Evelyn Noble

Fig. 29 Headstone Of Noble Family In Malvern Wells Cemetery

Fig. 30 Headstone Of Burcher family In Malvern Wells Cemetery

2.13 Electoral Register Entries (1965 to 1967)

The Electoral Register Entries for 1965, 1966 and 1967 are shown in Table 1. It is currently not known which of these, if any, were owners of The Clans Hotel.

Table 1 Electoral Register Entries 1965-1867

1965	1966	1967
Cyril A. Need	Arthur A. Buckley	John B. McDougal
Mabel D. Need	Pearl G. Buckley	Bertha W. H. McDougal
Charles Prior	John B. McDougal	John P. McDougal
Camilla Pammer	Bertha W. H. McDougal	Arthur E. Hathaway
---	John P. McDougal	---
---	Maria C. Elliot	---
---	Arthur E. Hathaway	---

Anne Noble was unable to say who owned the property at the time, but she reported that someone who had visited during this period had told her that the property was in a very rundown state.

2.14 Annie Millicent Comont, formerly Serjent, nee Boulton (Hotel St. Clare, 1968 To 1969)

Annie Millicent Boulton was born on the 21st of February 1899 at Broadway, Worcestershire. Her parents were Thomas Boulton, (born on the 5th of December 1869 at Little Comberton, Worcestershire, died on the 22nd of December 1934 at Aston Somerville, Broadway, Worcestershire), and Julia Sarah Bartlett, (born in 1870 at Oddington, Gloucestershire, died in December 1905 at Aston Somerville, Broadway, Worcestershire). Annie Millicent was the fifth child of nine, seven girls and two boys.

On the 31st of March 1901 she is recorded with her parents, five siblings and her grandmother Elizabeth Bartlett, living at Gorsepel Farm, Broadway where her father was a Stockman. Her mother died in 1905 after the birth of three more children, and her father went on to marry Martha Jane Bedwell of Naunton, Gloucestershire in 1907.

On the 2nd of April 1911 they are recorded as living in Aston Somerville where Thomas Boulton is recorded as a Waggoner on a farm. His eldest daughter, Emily May, is recorded in service to widower George Hunt at 33 Bridge Street, Evesham where she was employed as Cook. She died in 1915 age 25.

The second daughter Anne Elizabeth was not recorded with the family and has not been identified on the 1911 census. Two children born to Martha are recorded and there were to be further children born in 1912 and 1915 making a total of thirteen children in all. There was another early death; Mary Ann Boulton born 1897 died in 1920 age 23.

After leaving school about 1913 Annie Millicent learnt about the catering trade by working as assistant to Mrs Calloway and Miss Halliwell at St. Patrick's Tearoom in Broadway Worcestershire. In about 1917 she moved with them as a 'live-in assistant' when they went to The White Tearooms in High Street, Worcester. She was later joined by her two younger sisters, Ellen Julia and Blanche Margaret, who continued to live and work there until they married. Anna Pugh recalls her Aunt telling her that Elgar used to visit The White Tearooms for coffee and 'he always left a three penny tip', considered a good sum in those days.

In April 1922 Annie Millicent Boulton married for the first time, to James Frederick Serjent but this marriage was short lived; the actual date of the breakdown is not known but he went on to marry Evas M. E. McClean early in 1932.

It was during her first marriage that Annie Millicent began her own catering career and many changes of dwelling; with the assistance of memories of their visits to 'Aunt Nan' at her many establishments, Anna Pugh and her cousin Gill have drawn up a possible list of the many and rapid changes of location.

Anna describes her aunt as 'a very feisty lady who was great fun to be with'; also she often had a number of her nieces to stay with her and was extremely tolerant with them. She had no children of her own, something she regretted.

Her first experience of her own business was when she ran the Priory Tea Rooms in Church Street, Malvern in 1929 - 1930 while still married to James Serjent; Anna believes that they lived on the premises.

On the 20th of April 1935 at the Registry Office in Barton under Irwell, Lancashire, Annie Millicent married James Geoffrey Comont, recorded as an 'Automobile Electrician' (possibly an A.A. man) of Victoria Road, Stretford, Lancs. Her address at the time was given as 33 Court Road, Malvern and she was working as a 'Confectioner's Assistant'. For some unknown reason her name was recorded on the marriage certificate as 'Annie Elizabeth otherwise

Annie Millicent Serjent, formerly Boulton'; she signed the register as 'A. E. Serjent'. There is a suggestion that she did not like the name Millicent.

Between 1942 and 1945, Anna reports that she remembers visiting 'Aunt Nan' in Manby Road but in 1945, as recorded in the Telephone Directory, Annie Millicent and James Comont moved to Cleveland House, Priory Road, Malvern which they renamed 'The Sherington Hotel'; this is now Sherington House, 44 Priory Road, Malvern. For the next ten years Annie Millicent continued to run the Sherington Hotel; electoral registers show that Annie and James Comont were both present up until 1951.

This marriage was also to end in divorce; James is known to have remarried in Malvern in 1956 and moved to Pershore, where he is listed in telephone directories at 4 Farways Walk, Whitcroft Road, Pershore; he died there in 1977.

Annie continued to run the Sherington Hotel herself, with the services of her cook and 'general dogsbody' Bridget Gannon, until 1956; Anna is unable to say exactly when Bridget joined Annie but refers to her as 'always being there'. Commenting on the 'back problem' for which Bridget required 'medication', she recalls her mother saying that 'Aunt Nan was enough to drive anyone to drink!'

Anna and Gill remember being 'invited to visit' on numerous occasions when they knew that they would be required to help prepare and serve at wedding receptions that were often held at the hotel. During her adult life, this period at the Sherington Hotel was to be the longest time that Annie Millicent spent at any one address; over the next twenty years she seems to have moved either home or business almost every year.

There followed a brief period at The Bay Tree Hotel, now Priory House, 38 Priory Road, Malvern. Anna clearly remembers being asked to visit to help with clearing the building, commenting particularly on the removal of 'an extremely dirty stair carpet'.

Annie Millicent then moved to 27 Wyche Road where she is recorded in the telephone directory for 1958 and 1959 before taking over The Holdfast Hotel at Welland between 1960 and 1961. 1962 to 1963 sees her living at 11 Alexandra Road, Malvern, as recorded in the telephone directory, and it is during this time that Anna believes she ran The Blue Bird Tea Rooms at 9 Church Street Malvern.

Memories seem rather hazy at this point, but both Anna and Gill remember their Aunt living briefly in Graham Road, Malvern, before moving to Roebuck House, Madresfield Road in 1964 to 1965. She then ran The Abbey Tearooms in Church Street Malvern in 1966 to 1967; this is believed to have been in the same building as the Priory Tea Rooms referred to in 1930.

In conversation with Anna she described this as being more or less opposite the gates to Malvern Priory and set back from the road, the position now occupied by the Anupam Indian Restaurant. It is suggested that at this time Aunt Nan was living in Victoria Park Road, Malvern Link.

Annie Millicent, still with the services of Bridget Gannon as Cook, bought 34 Priory Road, Malvern and ran it as Hotel St. Clare in about 1968. The electoral register for 1968 and 1969 lists Annie Comont and Bridget Gannon with three permanent residents, Margaret McGregor, Colonel George Whitworth and Jack Wilcox. Margaret McGregor was the grandmother of Joyce Howard, nee Webster who was destined to become the next owner of Hotel St. Clare.

By this time she was 70 years old and, although the hotel had a full order book for the coming season, Annie Millicent decided to offer it for sale to Joyce Howard following one of her regular Sunday lunch visits to her grandmother.

As a result Annie moved to 28 Abbey Road, Malvern, where she is recorded from 1969 until 1970, before moving to 48 Cedar Avenue, Malvern Link until at least 1972. No record was found in the telephone directories from 1972 to 1975, when she is recorded at 19 Nursery Road, Malvern. The final entry found for her was in 1976 at 4 Greenfield Road, Malvern Link which proved to be her last permanent address.

Annie Millicent died at Court House Nursing Home, Court Road, Malvern on the 3rd of February 1979, aged 80. The cause of death, certified by G A Flann M.D., was given as chronic heart failure; the death was registered by Annie Tulip Fairs of Grosvenor House, Church Street, Malvern but the certificate does not indicate her relationship to Annie Millicent.

She was buried on the 9th of February 1979 in Grave No L11 E 25 in Malvern Cemetery, Madresfield, Road, Malvern. The grave is marked by a black marble headstone with the inscription:

'In loving Memory, Annie Millicent Comont 1899 - 1979 R I P'.

Photographs of Annie Millicent have kindly been provided by Anna Pugh.

Fig. 31 James Geoffrey Comont and Annie about 1935

Fig 32 Annie Millicent Comont about 1968

Fig. 33 The Headstone Of Annie Comont In Malvern Cemetery

2.15 Joyce Margaret Howard, nee Webster (Hotel St. Clare, 1969 to 1972)

Joyce was happy to provide personal details of herself and her family, but records of these will be limited since many of the members are still living.

Joyce Margaret Webster was born on the 27th of May 1936 in Aberdeen, Scotland; the eldest child of John William England Webster, (born on the 21st of April 1908 at 89 Sunnyside, Aberdeen, Scotland, died at Worcester in May 1989), and his wife Margaret, (born June 1911 at St. Machar, Aberdeen, Scotland, died at Malvern, Worcestershire in January 1986).

At the time her father was a General Medical Practitioner in Aberdeen, and during the war he served in the Royal Army Medical Corps at Dunkirk and in India. Joyce and her mother lived at Cairnbaan, Aberdeen, where her father joined them, when he was demobilised, and continued in medical practice.

It was to be a happy accident that brought the family to Malvern. It was usual at that time for doctors to purchase their practices and John Webster replied to a particular advertisement in the British Medical Journal for a place that interested him; as was usual the address was given as a box number. He received a reply from old Dr. Meikle of Malvern, although it was not where he had applied; he later found that the envelope had been in the rain and the box number had been smudged.

After checking where Malvern was situated Joyce's father decided that he would visit the area and, liking what he found, he decided to purchase the practise from Dr. Meikle at St. Michael's, Worcester Road, Malvern, Worcestershire. The family moved to Malvern in 1946 and Joyce remembers that, as the practice was situated at the family home, she was required to be on her best behaviour at all times; something which, she suggested, did not come easily to her.

She was sent to Clarendon School in Hornyold Road, Malvern, which she recalls was run by ladies belonging to the Plymouth Brethren. They were very strict, and Joyce was extremely unhappy there; when the school was due to move to new premises in 1947 she told her parents that she was not prepared to move with them and she was sent to a Miss Lawson in St. Andrews Road, Malvern. She was a private Governess who tutored five pupils in her own home; Joyce spent a much happier year with her. She said that her parents had applied for a place at Malvern Girls College but this was refused, she suggested that this was because her father was considered to be 'trade'.

After her year with Miss Lawson, in 1948, Joyce moved to Douglas House School, (formerly known as 'The Slopes' and later 'Prior's Mount') which was situated in Priory Road in the grounds opposite St. Ronan's, now belonging to Malvern College. The building no longer exists, the Art Block being built in that area, but the tennis courts behind the Art Block, visible from the gated entrance in Priory Road, are known to this day as 'Douglas House Courts'.

Winstanley, the house which preceded Crellin House, was used as a boarding house and Head teacher's residence for Douglas House School. Joyce recalls that when she was there, the Head Mistress was Mrs Owen Williams; she attended this school for four years leaving in 1952 aged 16.

At that time she had obtained a place at St. Bartholomew's Hospital, London, to study nursing when she was 18 years old. Her mother very wisely insisted that, rather than stay at home for two years, she should attend Worcester Technical College, Victoria Institute, taking a one year course in Domestic Science, and one year Secretarial Training; both of these were to become essential in Joyce's later life.

Joyce readily admits that she knew nothing about running a home and cooking was totally new to her; there had always been a cook at the house as she grew up. She tells how she caused mayhem in the Domestic Science Department, nearly causing a fire when she burnt pans dry, but she managed to complete the year and move on to the Secretarial course.

Very early in her time at the Technical College, when still only 16, Joyce met a young man on a bus named Michael Howard and she says that she knew straight away that he would become her husband. As a result she never took up her place to study nursing and instead, in 1955, took a Secretarial post at the Royal Radar Establishment in Malvern, later to become QinetiQ.

In July 1958, Joyce married Michael Lawrence Howard at Malvern Priory. At the time Michael was doing his National Service and they lived in a caravan on the Caravan Park, Hanley Swan, but after two months of being 'a weekend wife' she obtained a transfer to Boscombe Down, Wiltshire and found someone to tow the caravan to a new site closer to her husband.

After Michael was demobbed they moved to Berkshire and in March 1961 their first child, a son, was born. After this they moved to Camberley in Surrey where their eldest daughter was born in July 1963, followed by another daughter in May 1965.

Tragically Michael Lawrence Howard died suddenly in September 1965, following an aneurism; he was 33 years old, and Joyce was left at the age of 29 with a baby of four months and two other children under five. She returned to Malvern to her parents in a state of total shock and for the next two years they lived in a large caravan at her parent's home while Joyce came to terms with life as a single parent, gradually realising that she would have to find a way of supporting herself and her children.

Electoral Registers show that in 1968, Joyce's grandmother, Margaret McGregor, was a permanent resident at Hotel St. Clare, Priory Road Malvern, with Annie Millicent Comont. Joyce regularly took the children to have Sunday lunch with Great Grandma and on one occasion she recalls Mrs Comont 'inviting her into her private sitting room'; she was sure that she was going to be told that the children were too ill behaved and that she should not bring them to lunch again.

Instead, Mrs Comont told her that she was looking to give up the hotel, which had a full order book for the coming year, and suggested that, as she knew Joyce needed to find a means of supporting herself and her family, she should buy Hotel St. Clare from her. Joyce had never had any experience of running a business or catering for a number of people, but she asked for 24 hours to think it over, after which she agreed and bought the Hotel as a going concern, complete with Cook, for £10,000 (£140,000 at 2012 values).

Joyce gave a very lively account of life at Hotel St. Clare from 1969-1972, her many anecdotes being reminiscent of a script from 'Fawlty Towers'. At first she had the services of the cook, Bridget Gannon, and two part time ladies, Mrs Hall who came in to change beds and Mrs Kennedy to clean. There was also a gardener who looked after the outside area, but eventually she was running the hotel with the help of only Mrs Hall and Mrs Kennedy.

When Joyce took over in 1969, in addition to her grandmother, Margaret McGregor, who occupied a single room at the front of the building, there were a number of other permanent residents including Colonel George Whitworth, who occupied the single room in the tower approached by a separate staircase, Jack Wilcox and several other elderly ladies for whom there is no record.

It seems that the children enjoyed their time at St. Clare, amassing a 'menagerie' of creatures that were kept in the small courtyard at the rear of the building, including 'Dandelion' – a white, man eating rabbit with escapist tendencies which required frequent chases round the garden to enable it's recapture, much to the amusement of the residents.

On one occasion Joyce was required to pay for a new pair of trousers for a delivery man who had been 'savaged' by Dandelion. Eventually the rabbit was seen sitting in the middle of the road, Joyce was serving lunch and by the time she went outside it was no longer to be seen; she was later told that it had been 'picked up by gypsies and was living happily in West Malvern'.

In 1970 her grandmother had a fall and died soon afterwards. Following the loss of another of her old ladies, who was found dead in her bed one morning, Joyce decided on a change and advertised vacancies at her old employers, RRE, hoping to find some younger male clients. As a result Roy Williams and Harold Sutcliffe took up residence at St. Clare after their previous accommodation at Granta Lodge was closed down.

The inherited cook, Bridget Gannon, was born in Ireland on the 8th of February 1913; she was described as a 'very good cook – most of the time'; unfortunately Bridget had a 'back problem' that required frequent 'medication' that was taken in her room. It was some time before Joyce realised the extent of the problem; Bridget became increasingly unreliable and the situation came to a head on the day that the teachers from Hillside School, attended by Joyce's three children, were booked for lunch following the School's Prize Giving.

Having taken time off to attend the event Joyce returned to find that, although everything was prepared, no cooking had been done and Bridget was apparently asleep in her room. After settling her guests down with a couple of bottles of sherry, she set to and cooked the meal herself. Bridget, refusing to accept any treatment for her alcohol problem, left her employment at the hotel. She died in Malvern in 1974 aged 61.

An advertisement in 'The Lady' magazine led to the appointment of a new cook, Mary, but she left in the middle of the night after just two weeks, without picking up any pay. From this point on Joyce undertook all the cooking herself with assistance from her two part time ladies. Unexpected and unwanted problems with the plumbing one day saw her cooking the meal wearing a sou'wester while one of the ladies held an umbrella over the stove!

She also lost the services of her gardener but, undaunted, she purchased what she believes was probably one of the 'earliest Flymo's in Malvern' and, after serving lunch to the residents, went out to mow the sloping lawn herself. The mower hit something, and afraid to let it go, Joyce found herself cart wheeling into the flowerbed. When she opened her eyes she was surrounded by a circle of concerned residents, one of whom begged her 'to promise not to mow the lawn again'. From then on Roy Williams took over the lawn mowing and flowerbeds, and Harold Sutcliffe took charge of the vegetable garden.

During the time that Joyce was running Hotel St. Clare, she was fortunate enough to make a profit the first year, but this was followed by two years of loss. These results, in addition to the stress of bringing up three lively children whilst trying to run a business, began to take a toll on her health. However, Harold Sutcliffe proposed marriage to Joyce – she says she wondered if, as a bachelor of 50, he knew what he was taking on; she accepted his proposal, but Harold insisted on asking the children for their permission also, something that was given very readily.

Joyce and Harold Keith Sutcliffe (born on the 1st of November at Oswaldthwistle, Lancashire) were married from Hotel St. Clare in

May 1972. They set up a new family home in Malvern where they spent all their married life, and St. Clare was sold to Dennis and Margaret Tatler for £13,500 (£162,000 at 2012 values).

Harold Sutcliffe died at the age of 81 in December 2003. Joyce continues to live in Malvern and is an active member of Malvern U3A.

Joyce is justifiably very proud of the achievements her three children, all of whom decided to follow careers in different areas of the medical profession – her son as a doctor, now very well known for his work in Old Age Psychiatry, her eldest daughter who specialised in intensive care, and her younger daughter who became a physiotherapist.

Joyce owned Hotel St. Clare from 1969 to 1972 and was the last person to run the building as a hotel.

Fig. 34 The information card for Hotel St. Clare circa 1969, provided by Joyce Sutcliffe

```
Telephone                                    Telegrams
   MALVERN 4717                              Hôtel St Clare


        Hôtel St. Clare

              14 PRIORY ROAD
                  MALVERN
               WORCESTERSHIRE


 Station                          Resident Proprietors
   GREAT MALVERN                     MRS. E. M. HOWARD
```

"Hôtel St. Clare"
possesses an unrivalled and secluded position facing south. It is centrally situated and stands in its own grounds, from which one can enjoy magnificent views of the hills and surrounding countryside.

The hotel, which is about seven minutes walk from Great Malvern station, and within a few minutes of the Winter Gardens, Priory Park, Festival Theatre, Swimming Pool and Shopping Centre, is very convenient for both the Malvern Boys and Girls Colleges.

Central heating throughout the hotel.
Comfortable, well furnished public rooms.
T.V., Reading Lounge. Pleasant Dining Room.
Bedrooms have H. and C. and interior sprung mattresses.
Modern Bathrooms.
Noted for good food and personal service.
Ample Parking facilities.
Open throughout the year to residents and non-residents.

2.16 Dennis Harold Tatler & Margaret Shirley Tatler (Tower House, 1972 to 1985)

In 1972 Denis and Margaret Tatler bought Hotel St. Clare from Joyce Sutcliffe and its use was changed from that of a hotel to a family home. At some point after this they renamed it Tower House. They are recorded there in the electoral register for 1973.

Although the Planning Application system began in 1948 the first planning application for Tower House was submitted in 1980. Details of applications made by the Tatlers are given below (Table 2). At this time they were Directors of a Computer Consultancy employing 4 staff and Tower House was stated as owned by the Tatlers with a mortgage.

Although the council finally approved their plans in January 1982 they were never carried out and the house was sold in 1985.

Fig. 35 Drawing of Tower House about 1972 by Margaret Tatler.

Table 2 Planning Applications Made By The Tatlers

Ser.	Application	Date	Applicant	Topic
1	80 / 01647	19th Jan 1980	Dennis H. Tatler	Two rooms used as offices
2	82 / 00100 / FUL	23rd Jan 1982	Dennis H. Tatler	Further offices
3	82 / 00101 / LBC	23rd Jan 1982	Dennis H. Tatler	Demolition of outbuildings. Re-build with pantry, offices and toilets

Application 80/01647 was made on the 19th January 1980 by Dennis Harold Tatler and Margaret Shirley Tatler to use two rooms of the house as offices.

They believed that use of the building as commercial premises would generate sufficient revenue to meet the heavy financial burden of maintaining the property.

The planning office considered the application a material change from residential to business use, and therefore planning permission would be required from the Council.

At this time Tower House was described as having 10 bedrooms and 4 reception rooms on 3 floors plus an attic. The Planning Application gives a plan of the ground floor of Tower House at that time.

Planning Application 82/00100/FUL, the 23rd January 1982, requested demolition of outbuildings, construction of new outbuildings for office accommodation, and a laundry and pantry for the main building, and conversion of part of the ground floor of Tower

House into computer offices. Planning permission was granted on the 25th January 1982.

Application 82/00101 was also made by Dennis H. Tatler on the 23rd January 1982 to demolish outbuildings and replace with a pantry, offices and a toilet.

In 1985 the Tatlers sold Tower House to Limbrick Developments Limited

3. Planning Applications Submitted after 1885

A number of speculative planning applications were made, not necessarily by the owner of the property.

3.1 Miss C Ward

Miss C. Ward of the School Bungalow, Warndon, Worcestershire submitted Planning Application 85/01340/FUL on the 15th July 1985 for change of use for Tower House to a nursing or convalescent home.

Miss Ward intended to purchase the property but withdrew the Application when the site was sold to Limbrick Developments Limited.

3.2 Limbrick Developments Limited

Limbrick Developments Ltd, Alfords Farm, Upleadan, Newent, Gloucester GL18 1EF, purchased Tower House in June 1985.

Limbrick submitted Planning Application 85/01790 on the 23rd August 1985 for change of use to a nursing home for elderly people. The application was approved.

Limbrick asked the planning authority for their view of demolition of Tower House and obtained the reply from the Malvern Hills Conservation architect that the 'building was not particularly meritorious and there would be no objection to demolition'.

Application 86/1722 described the building as vandalised and uninhabitable. Demolition was agreed on the basis that an acceptable re-development would be proposed and approved.

This Application described the ground floor as consisting of a main hall, an inner hall, four reception rooms, kitchen, larder, stores, utility room and cloakroom, having a total area of 140 square metres.

The first floor was described as consisting of stairs and landing, five bedrooms, one bathroom and a WC, having a total area of 120 square metres.

The second floor was described as consisting of stairs, narrow passageway to five bedrooms, bathroom and WC, having a total area of 120 square metres.

The building had extensive dry rot from the cellar to the roof timbers. Rentokil remedial work was quoted as £37,677 (£94,192 at 2012 values) plus VAT. A surveyor estimated the total restoration costs as £150,000 (£375,000 at 2012 values).

At this time the building was derelict with scaffolding erected and no rates being paid.

Planning Application 87/02137/FUL was submitted on the 14th September 1987 for a building consisting of 15 two bedroom flats as sheltered housing.

The Application was refused in October 1987 but allowed on appeal in April 1988. The development did not proceed.

3.3 Bovis Homes

Planning Application 87/02138/FUL, made by Bovis Homes Ltd on the 14th September 1987, was a continuation of the previous Application. They probably acquired Tower House during the first 6 months of 1988.

A tree report was commissioned from Roy Finch and Bovis stated their intention to demolish Tower House by December 1988.

On the 25th of October 1988 Bovis instructed Demolition (Maypole) Ltd, of Hall Green, Birmingham B28 0SX to demolish Tower House.

Demolition began on Monday the 7th November with planning permission for a 4 or 6 storey block of retirement apartments.

The site was then scrub-land until the building of Priory Gardens began in 1999. However between 1989 and 1998 Bovis continued to make planning applications.

Planning Application 89/0361 was made on the 10th February 1989 by Bovis Homes, Lansdown Road, Cheltenham, for an increase in the number of car parking spaces.

The application was for 15 two bedroom flats and 12 parking spaces. The A, B, C and D wings were very different from the design of Tower House. Approval was granted on appeal in April 1989, including consent to demolish Tower House.

Bovis Retirement Homes submitted Planning Application 91/00770/FUL on the 23rd May 1991 for retirement housing with 18 units.

Approval was granted for 18 two bedroom units, with 27 car parking spaces. Bovis changed the Application from retirement homes to flats for general use in Application 1994/00689/FUL on the 10th June 1994.

Application 1997/01221/FUL made on the 23rd of September 1997 for 18 flats was refused on the 2nd December 1997.

Bovis submitted Planning Application 98/00929/FUL on the 11th August 1998 for 15 flats. The application was refused with a maximum of 12 flats allowed.

The first land registry act was passed in 1862 but land registration did not become compulsory until 1990 when the records were also made accessible to the public.

Registration of land in the Bromsgrove and Worcester regions began in 1977. The first freehold registration of the land at 34 Priory Road in 1998 was submitted by Marchfield Estates (South) Ltd and given the Title Number HW87370, dated 16th February 1998.

Subsequent enquiries with the Land Registry indicate that no supporting documentation is available. Consequently 160 years of Deeds, plans and historical records appear to be untraceable.

The house immediately opposite to Tower House was Winstanley and was demolished at about the same time. Winstanley was suffering from subsidence to the point where the lift could no longer be used.

The following photographs were kindly contributed by Roger Hall-Jones.

Fig. 36 Tower House shortly before demolition November 1988

Fig. 37 Winstanley at the Time of Demolition. November 1988

4. Priory Gardens

4.1 Construction

Priory Gardens was constructed by Harper Group Construction Limited of Rowley Regis.

Planning consent was granted on the 9th July 1999 on the basis that many of the Victorian features of Thorpe House would be incorporated into Priory Gardens. The chimneys, for example, are decorative and non-functional. Building construction commenced on the 16th November 1999 with an estimated construction time of 54 weeks (July 2000)

The site area was given as 0.3 Hectares of waste ground. Local residents report that foxes and badgers were resident on the site at that time.

The following photograph was kindly contributed by Eluned Ellis.

Fig. 38 Priory Gardens Site At The Start Of Construction

The building was constructed using Ibstock Kennett Orange Blendare bricks with imitation concrete stone trimming.

The entire stone wall frontage was re-built using a concrete block wall clad with the dressed stones from the original wall.

The construction time for Priory Gardens was 2 years; twice as long as the estimated time of 54 weeks stated in the planning application.

Doreen Howes was the first resident of Priory Gardens and took up occupation in June 2001. All 15 flats were sold by April 2002.

The following photograph was kindly contributed by Helen Irwin.

Fig. 39 Priory Gardens 2001

2. Purchase of the Freehold

Due to dissatisfaction with the standard of the existing property management the residents decided to purchase the Freehold from Marchfield Estates (South) Ltd.

Progressing of the purchase was undertaken by Louis D. Thomas. A valuation of the freehold was obtained from a chartered surveyor at a cost of £575-00 who valued the freehold at £25,000.

Russells Solicitors of Church Street Malvern were appointed to complete the legal requirements of the purchase.

Priory Gardens (Malvern) Limited was incorporated on the 17th November 2005, with number 05626276, as the company making the offer for the freehold. The Accounting date was 30th September, commencing 30th Sept. 2008 as the reference.

Twelve of the fifteen flats chose to become members of PG(M) Ltd and meet the cost of purchasing the freehold equally between them.

The freehold was purchased from Marchfield for £27,500 in November 2006. This figure was near the rule-of-thumb calculation method of 15 times the ground rent (15 times 15 flats times £120 = £27,000).

Philip, Laney & Jolly were appointed as the managing agents and also as the Secretary of PG(M) Ltd.

Discussions about purchasing the freehold began in June 2004 with the purchase being completed in November 2006 and throughout the 18 month period Philip Laney & Jolly provided advice and support. By 2012 all leaseholders had become members of Priory Gardens (Malvern) Limited.

Appendix A1 Names of Adjacent Properties in Priory Road.

Num.	Current Name	Previous name/s	
44	Sherington House	1861	Cleveland House
		1950	Sherington Hotel
42	Landsdowne Court	1854	Osbourne House
		1884	The Vicarage
40		1861	Tibberton House
	---	1903	Southbury
			Russeldene Hotel
38	Priory House	1854	Chalford
		1884	Lystonville or Lyonsville
		1960's	Bay Tree Hotel
36	St. Ronan's		
34	Priory Gardens (2nd building)	1853	Thorpe House
		1856	St. Clare
		1948	St. David's Hotel
		1950	The Clans Hotel
		1967	Hotel St. Clare
		1972	Tower House
32	Portswood		
30	Priory Court (2nd building)	1854	Cranhill
		1911	Bryndart
		1940	Musgrave
28	Priory Court (2nd building)	1861	Clydesdale
33	Crellin House (2nd building)	1884	Winstanley
	Malvern College Art Department	1854	The Slopes
		1901	Prior's Mount
		1950	Douglas House School

Appendix A2 Malvern Cemeteries

A2.1 Great Malvern Cemetery, Madresfield Road, Malvern, Worcestershire

The occupiers of the property who are buried in Malvern Cemetery

	Name	Cemetery Reference	Map Reference (Fig 40)
1	Edward Ratheram	Grave Number 1797, Plot 4	H6
2	Harriet Frances Ratheram	Grave Number 1797, Plot 4	H6
3	Amy East	Grave Number 4CP, 2623	G7
4	Charles Harry East	Grave Number 4CP, 2623	G7
5	Laura Margaret Owen	Grave Number CP, D12	G6
6	Annie Millicent Comont	Grave Number L11, E25	D5
7	John Henry Roper-Curzon	Grave Number 1223, Plot 3	H6
8	Harriet Roper-Curzon, and 'All Infant Children'.	Grave Number 1223, Plot 3	H6

The first burial in Malvern Cemetery was in 1841. The location of the first burial was determined by how much the executors were prepared to pay. The most expensive plots were those nearest to the Sexton's Office, currently the Lodge, as this location minimised the risk of grave robbing for the jewellery often buried with the deceased.

The reference 'CP' refers both to 'Chapel Plot' and also to 'Cremation Plot'. All location references have been provided by Malvern Town Council

Unlike burials in Church grounds, burials in Council Cemeteries are assigned indefinitely. There is a likelihood that this arrangement may change when space becomes limited.

The cemetery recently purchased (Feb 2012) the allotments next to Madresfield Road. This, together with the remaining free land will provide space for burials for a further 30 years.

Also buried in the cemetery are Dr. Wilson, who brought the Water Cure to Malvern, the singer Jenny Lind and a number of the family of Alfred Speer, original owner of the building which replaced Dr. Gully's house, now known as The Council House.

Fig. 40 Plan of Malvern Cemetery

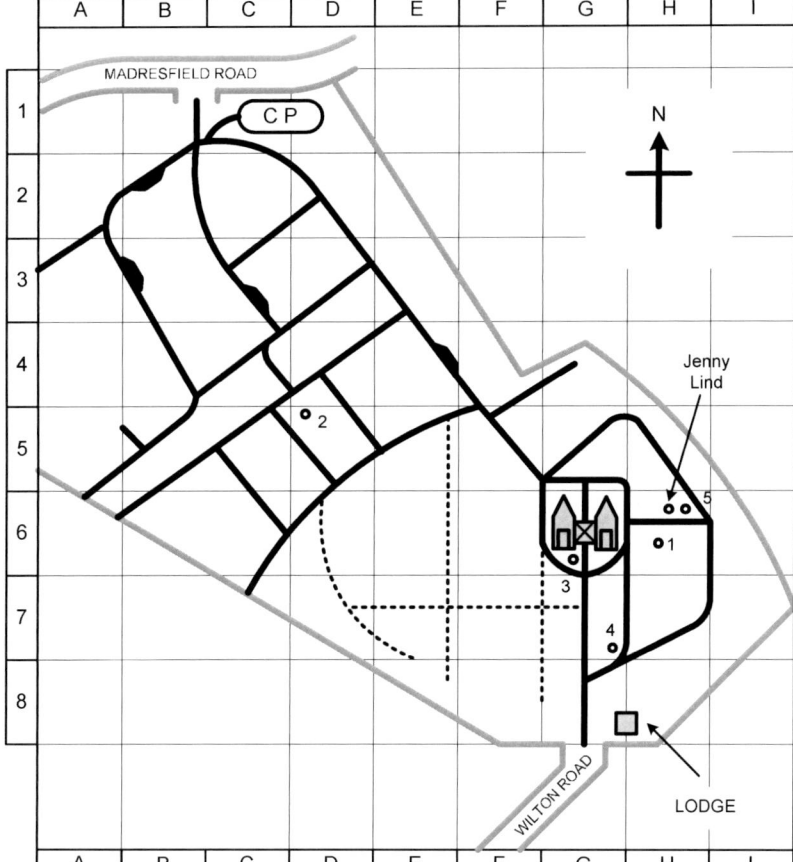

1. Edward and Harriet Ratheram.
2. Annie Comont.
3. Laura Margaret Owen.
   No headstone, immediately to the right of the headstone for Reg Lower
4. Amy East. Charles Harry Hangar East
5. John Henry Roper-Curzon. Harriet Ann Roper-Curzon and 'All Infant Children'.

A2.2 Malvern Wells Cemetery, Green Lane, Malvern Wells, Worcestershire

William Noble, Esme Maud Noble and Audrey Evelyn Noble are buried in Malvern Wells Cemetery in plot 1157. Their eldest daughter Margaret and her husband William Burcher are buried 2 plots further along the same row.

The first burials in Malvern Wells cemetery were in 1861. This is also the date when the Chapel in the cemetery was built.

Fig. 41 Plan of Malvern Wells Cemetery

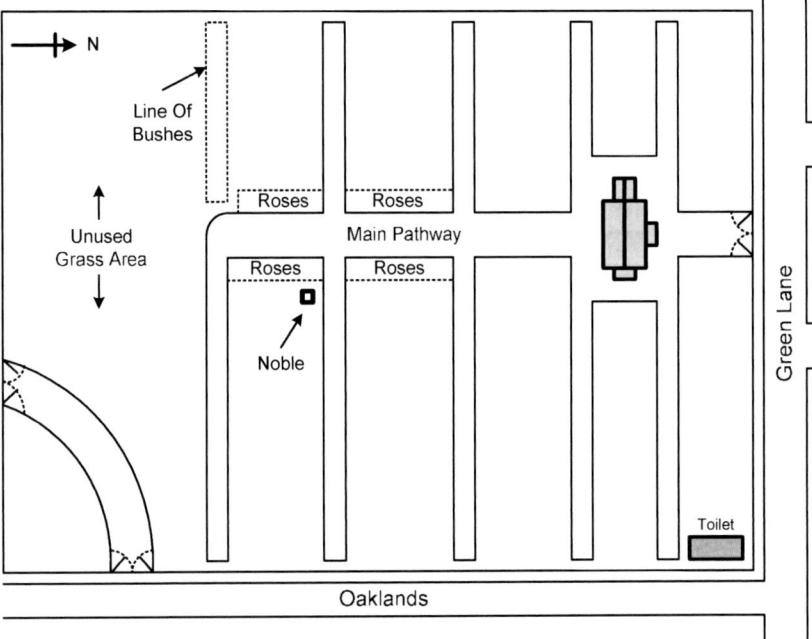

A2.3 St. James' Church Cemetery, West Malvern, Worcestershire

John Henry Dixon Phelps M.D. and his wife Lucy Olive Phelps are buried in the cemetery at St. James' Church, West Malvern.

His name is recorded on a head stone that also contains Reginald Parker (father in law), Reginald Irving Parker (brother in law), Margaret Irving Parker (mother in law) and Archibald Francis Robson, former vicar of St James' (brother in law).

On a smaller separate headstone are the names of Dorothy Anne Robson (sister in law) and Lucy Olive Phelps.

A third much smaller stone erected on the plot commemorates Phyllis Margaret Parker (infant sister in law) buried at Old Smethwick Cemetery and Anthony Irving Phelps (son) buried at Calgary, Canada

The original building on the site of St. James' Church was built in 1843. In 1869 it was demolished and replaced with the current building.

Dr Peter Mark Roget, M.D., F.R.S, (18th Jan 1779 to 1st Sept 1869, aged 91 years), best known for his work 'Roget's Thesaurus' is also buried in the grounds of St. James'.

His grave consists of a horizontal granite tomb aligned North South rather than the more usual East West.

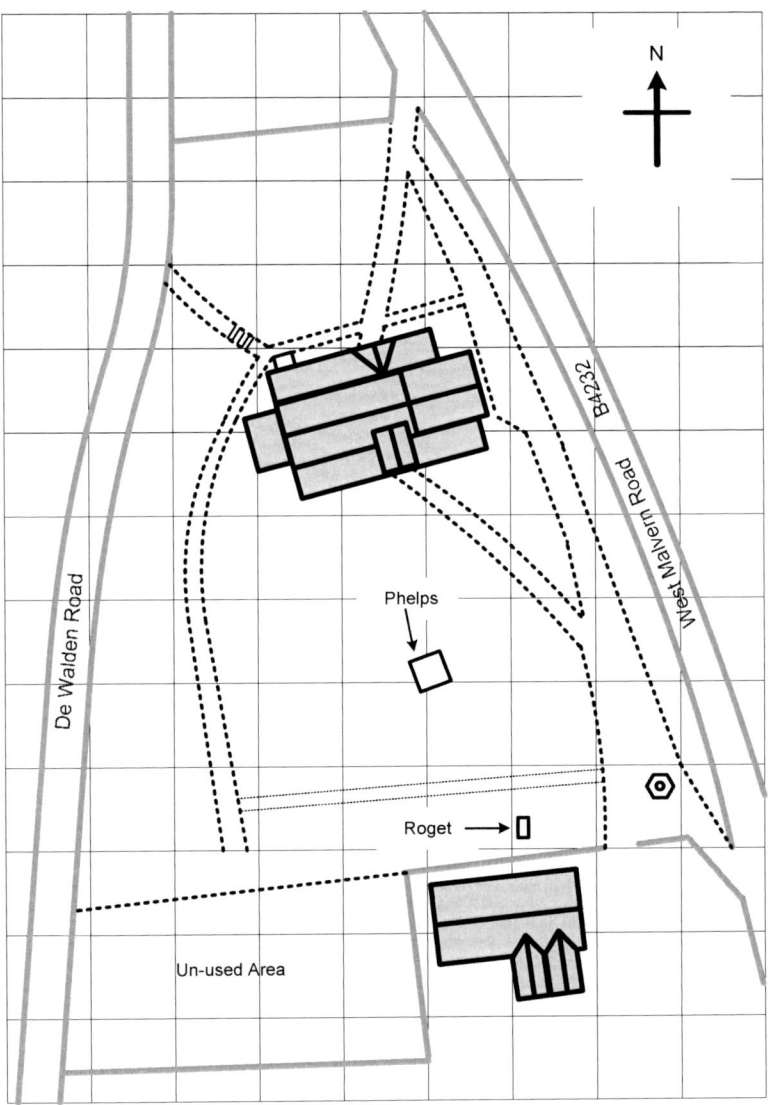

Fig. 42 Plan of St. James' Church Cemetery, West Malvern

Appendix A3 Sources of Information

Ancestry.com - www.ancestry.co.uk
- Birth, Baptisms, Marriage and Deaths, UK and Ireland, all records including General Records Office (GRO), Parish records & www.FreeBMD.
- Census records, UK 1841-1911, England and Wales Visitation
- Criminal Register – England and Wales.
- Directories for UK City, County & Trade, Crockford's Clerical, Medical Register, British Phone books 1880-1984.
- Education records including Cambridge Alumni, Oxford Alumni, Charterhouse Register, Harrow School Register, and Marlborough School Register.
- Electoral Rolls Australia & New Zealand
- Military Records – UK WW1 Service & Medal Rolls, Death records, Naval Casualties & War Graves, New Zealand WW1 Reserve Rolls, Royal Aero Club Aviators certificates.
- National Probate Calendar 1861-1941
- Newspapers – England, Andrews index 1790-1976
- Passenger Lists - UK incoming, US New York.
- Public Member Trees
- Rootsweb freepages – History, Religion (Lees Summit – Haefner) & Obituary index.

Bain, C W Curtis
- Obituary -Terence East

Barfoot, Peter
- Universal Directory of British Trade, Commerce and Manufacture Vol.2

Bray, Margaret
- Littlebury's Directory 1908, Kelly's Directory 1940 - Malvern Residents

BBC Hereford and Worcester
- 17 May 2010. Worcester to Hereford Railway

Blumenau, Ralph
- A History of Malvern College, 1865-1965

Birmingham Alphabetical List
- Birmingham residents

Birmingham Assay Office
- Edward Ratheram makers mark

British History Online
- Victoria County History

British Library. www.britishnewspaperarchive.co.uk
- Historical newspaper articles for Birmingham, Bristol, Worcester, etc.

BMA Journal
- Obituaries for medical practitioners

Bonham's Auctioneers, San Francisco, USA
- Sale notice of a cut-out silhouette of Harriet Ratheram

Cambridge University
- Peterhouse WW2 War Memorial

Canadian Virtual Memorial
- WW2 Memorial – Anthony Phelps

Church, Clare
- Electoral registers for Malvern

Church of Latter Day Saints, Utah, USA www.familysearch.org
- Parish Records of Baptism and Marriage

Commonwealth War Graves Commission
- Military deaths WW1 & WW2

Edinburgh Gazette
- Public and military announcements

Federation of Family History Societies
- National Burial Index

Find My Past. www.findmypast.co.uk
- Birth, Marriages and Deaths, UK – All records including GRO , Parish Records, Consular Records
- Census Records – UK 1841-1911
- Clergy List 1898
- Death Duty Registers 1796-1903
- Directories – Pigot's, Leeds; Kelly's Handbook 1910
- Medical Register 1913
- Military Records – East India Register 1855, Harts Army List 1888, WW1 Army Deaths, WW1 Navy Medal Rolls, WW2 RAF deaths.
- Passenger lists - leaving UK ports.

General Record Office
- Copies of Birth, Marriage, Death certificates

Giles, Adrian
- A Short History of Kitson's Pharmacy'

Historical Directories, Leicester University
- Various County Directories

Hutber, John & Carol
- Original deeds and other documents relating to St. Ronan's.

London Gazette
- Military announcements, Bankruptcies, Company information.

Malvern Hills District Council Planning Office
- Planning Applications

Malvern Hills Conservators
- Map of Malvern Oct 1854

Malvern Library
- Local Newspapers - microfilm

Malvern Town Council
- Burial Records Malvern Cemetery

Malvern Museum
- Drawing of Ordnance Survey map 1884

NARA Archives, USA
- US Census 1910, 1920

National Archives
- Birmingham City Archives – Mason family papers
- Recommendations for Honours and Awards
- Wills and Probate

Nichol, Rev. David
- Burial Records, St. James Church Cemetery

Ordnance Survey Commission
- Maps of Malvern area

Osborne, Bruce & Weaver, Cora
- Springs, Spouts, Fountains and Holy Wells of the Malvern Hills. 2012

Pall Mall Gazette
- Family announcements

Personal Communications
- Bairstow/Hiley Family – Peter Cole, Tony Cole
- Comont/Boulton Family – Jackie Powell, Anna Pugh
- East family – Sarah Horn(nee East)
- Howard family and Hotel St. Clare – Joyce Sutcliffe
- Noble family and The Clans Hotel– Anne Noble, John Noble, Angela Martell, Norman Brown, Alex Worswick

Pevsner, Nikolaus
- Worcestershire – The Buildings of England

Plantagenet Roll of the Blood Royal
- Roper Curzon family history

Photographs
- Tony Cole – Constance Bairstow
- Eluned Ellis – Priory Gardens Site 2000
- Roger Hall-Jones – Tower House and Winstanley
- Doreen Howes – Monumental Inscriptions
- Helen Irwin – Priory Gardens 2001
- John Noble – Hotel St. Clare, Noble family
- Anna Pugh – Annie Millicent Comont

Probate Office, Leeds
- Copies of Wills

Sale, Charles
- Gravestone Photographic Resource

Scotland's People. www.scotlandspeople.gov.uk
- All records of Scottish Births, Baptisms, Marriages and Deaths with copies of certificates

Sheffield Assay Office
- Ratheram Makers Marks

Smith, Brian
- A History of Malvern

Somerset Heritage Centre
- Wrington records

Taverner, David
- Burial Records Malvern Wells Cemetery

The Gentleman's Magazine
- Family announcements

The Times Online Archive
- Public and family announcements

thepeerage.com
- Family histories

Thomas, David A
- Canning Story 1785-1985

Veitch, H N
- Sheffield Plate, Its History.... etc

Wilkinson, Paul. www.sutton-in-craven.org.uk
- Sutton in Craven Village History

Worcester County Cricket Archive
- Playing history - Peter Phelps

Worcestershire Archives and Archaeology Service – The Hive, Worcester
- Electoral Rolls – Malvern, other local records.
- Absent Voters Stourbridge, Kidderminster & Bewdley 1919

Appendix A4. Local Newspapers

The original copies of the newspapers are held in bound form in the British Library. Malvern Library has microfilm copies of the Malvern newspapers but not the originals. The first printing press to be established in Worcester was in 1548.

Birmingham Newspapers

- Birmingham Daily Post, 4 December 1857 to 20 May 1918
- Birmingham Post, 21 May 1918 to 2 November 1956
- The Birmingham Post & Birmingham Gazette, November 1956 to 23 September 1964
- The Birmingham Post. 24 September 1964 to present

Worcester Newspapers

The Worcester newspaper is the oldest surviving newspaper in the world.

- Worcester Post-man. 1690 to 1709, irregularly. A news sheet, no existing copies.
- Worcester Post, 1722.
- Weekly Worcester Journal, 1730.
- Berrow's Worcester Journal, Oct. 11th 1753.
- Berrow's Worcestershire Journal, 1988

Malvern Newspapers

Malvern newspapers in date order:

- The Malvern Advertiser, Visitor's List and Pictorial Newspaper No 1. 16th June 1855.
- The Illustrated Malvern Advertiser, Visitor's List and General Weekly Newspaper. 23rd June 1855 to 20th Oct 1855.

There is then an 8 month gap due to the Malvern Illustrated Advertiser being published only during the summer months.

- The Malvern Advertiser, Visitor's List and General Weekly Newspaper. 23rd June 1856 to 6th Aug 1864.
- The Malvern News & Journal. 30th May 1860 to 24th May 1865. #1 to #261. (This may have been titled: The Malvern News and Three Counties Journal)
- The Malvern Advertiser, Visitor's List, Ledbury & Upton Chronicle. 13th Aug 1864 to 30th Nov 1907.
- The Malvern News. 31st May 1865 to 19th Nov 1938. #262 to #4163
- The Malvern Look-On: A Local and General Record of the Weeks Works. 24th Mar 1886 to 22nd Oct 1890. #1 to #240.
- The Malvern Link Observer. 19th Mar 1897 to 18th Feb 1898.
- The Malvern Gazette. 29th April 1898 to 26th Mar 1970. #1 to #5799
- The Malvern Graphic. 1st Mar 1909 to 1st July 1909. #1 to #5.
- The Malvern Gazette & Ledbury Reporter. 2nd April 1970 to 30th Nov 2001. #5800 to #7446.
- The Malvern Gazette. 7th Dec 2001 to Present (2012). #7447 to Present (2012).

Appendix A5. Trade Directories for Worcestershire and Malvern

Most of the Trade Directories shown below are available to view in the Malvern Library or online at www.ancestry.co.uk and www.historicaldirectories.org.

Some are available to purchase online www.parishchest.co.uk and www.genealogysupplies.com .

Date	Directory
1828/1829	Pigot's Directory Worcestershire
1835	Pigot's Directory Worcestershire
1835	Pigot and Co's National Commercial Directory - Worcestershire Section
1840-1841	Bentley's Directory Worcestershire
1841	Pigot's Directory Worcestershire
1847	Hunts Commercial Directory Of Worcestershire
1850	Kelly's (Post Office) Directory of Worcestershire
1850	Slater's Directory Of Worcestershire
1851	Lascelles & Co's Directory of Worcester & Neighbourhood
1851	Slater's Directory of Birmingham, Worcester & the Potteries, The Potteries (staffs) & Worcester
1855	Billing's Directory & Gazetteer of Worcestershire
1860	Post Office Directory Worcestershire
1860	Cassey's Directory Of Worcestershire
1865	Jones's Mercantile Directory of the Iron District of South Staffordshire and East Worcestershire. Great Malvern is not covered.
1870	Kelly's Directory of Worcestershire
1872	Post Office Directory Worcestershire
1872	Deighton's Directory Of Worcestershire
1873	Percy, Butchers Worcestershire and Malvern Directory
1873	Littlebury's Directory of the County Of Worcestershire
1876	Post Office Directory of Worcestershire
1879	Littlebury's Directory & Gazetteer of Worcester & District
1884	Kelly's Directory of Worcestershire

	1888	Kelly's Directory of Worcestershire
	1892	Kelly's Directory of Worcestershire
	1896	Kelly's Directory of Worcestershire
	1900	Kelly's Directory of Worcestershire
	1908	Littlebury's Directory of Worcester
	1912	Kelly's Directory of Worcestershire
	1914	Bennett's Business Directory for Worcestershire
	1924	Kelly's Directory of Worcestershire
	1928	Kelly's Directory for Worcestershire
	1932	Kelly's Directory for Worcestershire
	1940	Kelly's Directory for Worcestershire
	2011	Malvern College Directory, 1865 to 1924. (Currently in print on CD)

Index

1

133 Great Charles Street · *28, 31, 32, 33, 37, 38*
14th Baron Teynham · See Roper-Curzon Henry Francis
1st Baronet Bagge of Stradsett · See Bagge William

A

Abbey Road · *3, 5, 94, 115*
Admiralty WRNS Hostel · *99*
Archdale
    Charles Wells · *64*
    Margaret · *64*
Atkinson
    Emily Cottam · *53*
    Joseph Milner · *53*
Austin
    Alice Mary · *58*

B

Bagge
    Emelia Jane · *64*
    William · *64*
Bairstow
    Ann Elizabeth · *92*
    Elizabeth · See Ingilby Elizabeth
    Ellen · *92*
    James · *88–93*
    John · 89
    Mary Maria · *92*
    Matthew · *89, 90*
    Sarah · *90*
    Susannah · See Hooson Susannah
    Thomas · *89, 90, 91*
    Thomas jnr · *90*
    Walter · *90, 91*
Barker
    Alice Gray · *70*
    Christopher Dove · *70*
    Lily Adeline · *71*
    Mabel Gray · *70, 72*
Barnes
    Dr George · *39, 40*
Bartleet
    Solicitors · *30, 31*
Bartlett
    Elizabeth · *122*
    Julia Sarah · *122*
Bartlett's Buildings · *28, 42*
Bateman
    Charles Malcolm · *91, 92*
    Malcolm · *93*
    William Frederick · *92*
Bedwell
    Martha Jane · *122*
Berde
    Richard · *1*
Bett
    David Inches · *60*
    Elspeth Marion · *61, 62, 63*
    Francis Bourdillon · *61, 65, 66*
    Henry Bourdillon Imlach · *64, 65*
    Janet Smith · *60*
    Jessie Amelia · *61, 63*
    Lavinia Georgine · *62, 63,* See Bourdillon Lavinia Georgine
    Major General Henry Imlach · *60–62*

Margaret · *See* Archdale
    Margaret
    Margaret Lavinia · 61, 62
    Pleasance Margaret · *64, 65*
    Stafford Henry Imlach · *61, 63, 64*
    William · *60*
Boulton
    Anne Elizabeth · *122*
    Annie Millicent · *122, 123*, *See*
        Comont Annie Millicent
    Blanche Margaret · *123*
    Ellen Julia · *123*
    Emily May · *122*
    Julia Sarah · *See* Bartlett Julia
        Sarah
    Martha Jane · *See* Bedwell
        Martha Jane
    Mary Ann · *122*
    Thomas · *122*
Bourdillon
    Amelia Anne Augusta · *60, 61*
    Lavinia Georgine · *60*
    Stafford · *60, 61*
Bovis Homes Ltd · *141*
Bovis Retirement Homes · *142*
Bredin
    Captain Waldene Edgar · *77*
    Major Waldene Fitzwilliam
        Hutchison · *77*
    Norah Elizabeth P · *77*
Bridgend Temperance Hotel,
    Aberayron · *103*
Brislington House · *63*
British Hospital in Buenos Aires · *79*
Broadway · *122*
Brown
    Ann Harman · *57*
    Harriet Ann · *52*, *See* Roper-
        Curzon Harriet Ann
    Major John Harman
    Major John Harman · *57*
    Lucy Maria · *57*

Adelaide Keith · *58*
Frederick Lennox Harman · *58*
Major John Frederick Harman ·
    58
Buckley
    Arthur A · *121*
    Pearl G · *121*
Burcher
    Margaret · *See* Noble Margaret,
        See Noble Margaret
    William George · *116*

C

Cadbury
    Barrow · *42*
    Richard · *42*
Chadwick
    Sarah Cooper · *77*
Chaffers
    Norman Bairstow · *92*
Chaffers,
    Dr. Edward · *92*
Chalford · *13, 14, 19*
Chalybeate Spring · *5*
Cheadle Royal Hospital · *95*
Church Street · *3, 5, 11, 123, 125*
Clans Hotel · *110, 112, 116, 121*
Clarence Road · *5*
Clarkson
    Alfred Bairstow · *96*
Cleveland House · *70, 124*
Comont
    Annie Millicent · *113, 122–26,*
        132
    James Geoffrey · *123*
Corn Mill · *5*
Council House · *3, 11*
Court House Nursing Home · *126*
Cox
    Emma · *45, 46*

Cromack
   LAC H. C. · *83*

D

d'Avigony
   Julia · *54*
Dandelion
   rabbit · *133*
Dawson
   Edward · *48*
De Chevigny
   Julia · *See* d'Avigony
Dent
   John · *29*
   William · *29*
Devereux
   Dr Arthur C · *80*
Dixon
   Lucy Olive · *81*
   Sarah Maria · *78*
Dog Well' · *See* Chalybeate Spring
Donald
   Matthewman Hodgson · *52*
Douglas House School · *130*
Drew
   John · *110*
Duncan.
   Ethel Maud · *82*

E

Earl
   Frances · 31
   John · *31*
East
   Amy · *See* Rynd Amy
   Charles · *67*
   Charles Frederick Terence · *68, 69, 74–76*

Charles Harry Hanger · *67–72*
   Emma · *See* Hanger Emma
   Jonathan Simon · *76*
   Mabel Gray · *See* Barker Mabel Gray
   Muriel Leticia Luise · *See* Stein Muriel Leticia Luise
   Norah Kathleen Meliora · *68, 69, 76*
   Terence · *See* Est Charles Frederick Terence
Edwardson
   Gladys M · *114*
Electroplating · *32*
Elgar
   Edward · *70, 123*
Elkington
   George · *32*
Elliot
   Maria C · *121*
Elmley Castle · *See* Savage
Elmslie
   Alice Gray · *71, See* Barker Alice Gray
Enderley · *68*
Evans
   Abraham Llewellyn · *102*
   Arthur Goronwy · *101, 102, 103*
   Arthur Goronwy jnr · *102*
   Laura Margaret · *See* Owen Laura Margaret
   Llewellyn Lloyd · *102*
   Mary Kathleen · *101, 103*

F

Faulkener
   Amelia Anne Augusta · *See* Bourdillon Amelia Anne Augusta
Foley · *1*

Fox
    Dr Edward
    Fraserburgh · *106, 107, 110*

G

Gannon
    Bridget · *124, 125, 132, 133*
Garnes
    Thomas · *35*
Garside
    Mary · *91, 94*
Gibraltar House, Monmouth · *62, 63*
Grange Road · *11*
Great Charles Street, Birmingham. · *28*
Great Malvern Railway Station · *7*
Greenroyd Mill · *92, 93*
Griffith
    Elizabeth · *57*
    Rev Thomas Charles
Gull
    Sir William
Gully
    Dr James Manby · *6, 11*
Gutch
    Rev Robert

H

Hanger
    Emma · *67*
Hardwick
    Marie Theresa · *See* Hodgson Marie Theresa
Harper Group Construction Limited · *145*
Hathaway
    Arthur E · *121*
Hawkins,

Bridget · *See* Roper-Curzon Bridget
Heaton
    Bismark · *94, 97*
Hiley
    Constance Elizabeth · *87–97*
    Frederick · *88*, *See* Hiley Frederick Charles William
    Frederick Charles William · *96*
    Isabella · *See* Jessop Isabella
    Mabel · *88, 93, 97*
    Rev Alfred · *87, 88*
    Rev. Richard William · *87, 88*
    Richard · *87*
HMS Duke · *99*
Hodgson
    Colonel James: · *51*
    Isabella · *51*
    Marie Theresa · 51
Hogge
    Charles Wells · *See* Archdale Charles Wells
Holdfast Hotel · *125*
Holtye House · *61*
Hooman
    Jane · *46*
Hooson
    Susannah · *90*
Horn and Trumpet · *108*
Hotel St. Clare · *viii, 13, 24, 113, 125, 132, 134*
Howard
    Joyce Margaret · *See* Sutcliffe Joyce Margaret
    Michael Lawrence · *131*

I

Ingilby
    Elizabeth · *90*
Irving

Sarah · *79*
Washington · *79*

J

J. Drew & Sons Ltd, Perry Barr Mills · *111*
Jennings
    Joshua Robert · *92*
Jessop
    Isabella · *87*
    Thomas · *87*
Jewellery Quarter · *29, 32, 33*
Johnstone
    Janet Smith · *See* Bett Janet Smith
Jones
    Elizabeth · *See* Roberts Elizabeth
    Evan Rowland · *101, 102*
    Laura Margaret · *See* Owen Laura Margaret

K

Kennedy
    Elizabeth · *67*
Kilmer
    John · *See* Kilner John
Kilner
    John · *32, 33, 37*
Kings' College Hospital · *67, 74*
Kirkby
    Dorothy · *93*
Knott House · *89, 90, 94*
Knottesford
    Ann · *1*
    John · *1*

L

Lane
    Charles Pelham · *48, 49*
    Joseph · *48, 49*
    Sarah · *48*
    Thomas · *29, 39, 41, 42, 46, 48–49*
Leisten
    Clara L · *75*
Limbrick Developments Ltd · *140*
Lind
    Jenny · *55, 150*
Llanrhydd Churchyard · *95, 96*
Lloyd
    Mary Catherine · *102*
Lyndhurst · *91*
Lyndon
    George Frederick · *38, 42*
    Walter · *42*
Lyttleton · *19, 54*

M

Madras Staff Corps · *60, 61*
Makin
    Helen Elizabeth · *41, 43, 46, 48, 91*
    William · *39, 41, 43, 46*
Malvern Cemetery · *41, 44, 55, 56, 58, 69, 72, 73, 105, 126, 128, 149, 151*
Malvern College · *54, 70, 71, 99, 112, 130*
Malvern Community Hospital Lansdowne Crescent · *68, 69, 80*
Malvern Rural Hospital, Newtown · *68*
Malvern Wells Cemetery · *115, 116, 120, 152*

Malvernbury Nursing Home · *115*
Marchfield Estates (South) Ltd · *143, 147*
Mason
   James · *2, 5*
   Mary · *2*
   Oliver · *2*
   Philip · *2*
   Samuel · *2*
   William Wallis · *2*
Mason estate · *3, 5, 7*
McCann
   George · *14*
McClean
   Evas M. E · *123*
McDougal
   Bertha W. H · *121*
   John B · *121*
   John P · *121*
McGregor
   Margaret · *125, 132*
McRobin
   David · *89*
Meikle
   Dr. · *129*
Mildred
   Mary Kathleen · *See* Evans Mary Kathleen
   Ronald Henry · *103, 104*
Mill Lane · *5*
Millbrook, Albert Road South · *80*
Mitchell
   Mary · *68, 69*
Momber
   Albert Reginald Theodore · *70*
   Gustavus Albert · *70*
   Mabel Gray · *See* Barker Mabel Gray
   Rex · *See* Momber Albert Reginald Theodore
Monument House · *31, 33, 34*
Moundsley Hall · *29, 41, 46, 48, 49*

Muntz
   Devereux Shaw · *39*
   John Devereux · *39*

N

Nanson
   Caroline · *53*
   Edward James · *53*
   John · *53*
Need
   Cyril A · *121*
   Mabel D · *121*
Nether Court farmhouse · *3*
Newey
   Annie Rose · *110*
Noble
   Alexander · *106*
   Andrew · *106, 107*
   Audrey Evelyn · *110, 114, 115*
   Esme Maud · *21, 104, 118, See* Willetts Esme Maud
   Margaret · *109, 111, See* Trail Margaret
   William · *21, 115, 106–15, 118*

O

Oliver
   Elizabeth · *2*
   James · *1*
Orchard Road · *5*
Orwell Lodge · *79*
Owen
   Ann Catherine · *See* Richards Ann Catherine
   Griffith Rowland · *101–4*
   Jennie · *101*
   John · *101*
   Laura Margaret · *101–5*

Margaret · *101*

P

Pammer
    Camilla · *121*
Park View Apartments · *94*
Parker
    Dorothy Ann · *81*
    Lucy Olive · *79*
    Margaret Irving · *See* van Wart Margaret Irving
    Phyllis Margaret · *83*
    Reginald · *79, 80, 81*
    Reginald Irving · *81*
Pembridge · *96*
Perrott's Folly · *See* The Monument
Peterhouse, Cambridge · *82*
Phelps · *83*
    Anthony Irving · *80, 82–83*
    Anthony Irving jnr · *82*
    Dr John Henry Dixon · *26, 54, 78–81*
    John Reginald · *80, 84*
    Lucy Olive · *See* Parker Lucy Olive
    Marjorie Ann · *See* Taylor Marjorie Ann
    Monica Denison · *See* Smith Monica Denison
    Peter Horsley · *79, 80, 81, 82*
    Rev William Whitmarsh · *78*
    Rev. John · *78*
    Sarah Maria · *See* Dixon Sarah Maria
Piggestye Way. · *See* Mill Lane
Pilstone House, Llandogo · *61*
Pinnock
    William · *1*
Porter
    Harriot · *27*
Portswood · *13, 14, 18, 19, 24*
Prince
    Annie · *46*
Prior
    Charles · *121*
Priory Gardens · *11, 13, 23, 25, 113, 142, 145, 146*
Priory Gardens (Malvern) Limited · *147*
Priory Mansion · *11*, *See* Council House
Priory Park · *11*
Priory Road · *5, 7, 124*
Priory Tea Rooms · *123*
Priory Teas · *109*

Q

Queens' Chapel of the Savoy · *75*

R

Radnor House · *70, 71*
Ratheram
    Charles · *27, 28, 29, 30, 42, 48*
    Edward · *24, 26, 27–43, 44, 45, 48, 91*
    Elizabeth · *28*
    Harriet Frances · *26, 30, 31, 33, 34, 36, 37, 41, 44, 45–47, 48*
Richards
    Ann Catherine · *101*
Roberts
    Elizabeth · *102*
Robson
    Dorothy Ann · *See* Parker Dorothy Ann
    Rev Archibald Francis · *81*
Roget,
    Dr Peter Mark · *153*
Roper-Curzon

Alfred G M · *59*
Bridget · *50*
Gertrude · *53*
Harriet Ann · *55, 57–59*, See
   Brown Harriet Ann
Henrietta Maria · *51, 52*
Henry Francis · *50*
Isabella · *51, 52*
James Gerald · *51*
John Henry · *50–55, 57, 58*
Lucy · *51, 52, 53*
Margaret Sydney · *51, 52*
Mary Matilda · *See* Roper-Curzon
   Mary Nathalia
Mary Nathalia · *51, 52, 53*
Richard Henry · *51, 52, 53*
Rotheram
   Edward · *See* Ratheram Edward
Royd Hill · *89, 90, 91*
Rugeley
   The Station Hotel · *108*
Rynd
   Amy · *67, 69*
   Constance · *69*
   Elizabeth · *See* Kennedy Elizabeth
   Rev Henry Nassau · *67*

S

Sangster
   Alexander · *110*
Savage
   Thomas Byrche · *1*
   William · *1*
Sequoia Dendron Gigantean · *21, 24*
Serjent
   Annie Millicent · *See* Comont
      Annie Millicent
   James Frederick · *123*
Shaw
   Ann Perry · *48*

Caroline Julia · *39*
Charles · *39, 48*
Helen Elizabeth · *See* Makin
   Helen Elizabeth
Phoebe · *48*
Sherington House · *See* The
   Sherington Hotel
Shipman
   Rev Thomas Trafford · *52*
Simpson
   Mary · *48*
Smith
   Arthur Denison · *82*
   Ethel Maud · *See* Duncan Ethel
      Maud
   Monica Denison · *82*
   Rev Isaac Gregory
Southfields Road · *5, 7*
Spa Cottage · *5*
Speer
   Alfred · *11, 150*
Spencer
   George · 90
   John Bairstow · *90*
   Sarah · *See* Bairstow Sarah
Springfield · *88, 89, 96*
St James' Church Cemetery · *81, 153*
St Ronan's · *18*
St. Clare · *13, 14, 36, 37, 41, 43, 45,*
   49, 54, 55, 57, 61, 68, 84, 91, 95,
   96, 99, 100, 105, 135, 136, 137
St. Clare, Sandfield Park, Liverpool ·
   41, 43
St. David's Hotel · *13, 104, 112*
St. George's Hospital · *79*
St. Remo · *71*
St. Ronan's · *13, 14, 17, 19, 23, 36,*
   71, 100, 130
Stein
   Clara L · *See* Leisten Clara L
   Hans Eric · *76*
   Julius William · *75*

Muriel Leticia Luise · *75*
Rick · *76*
Zoe Beatrice · *75, 76*
Storridge School · *102, 103*
Sutcliffe
  Harold Keith · *133, 134, 135*
  Joyce Margaret · *21, 24, 125, 129–35*
Sutton Coldfield
  Beccles · *109, 110, 115*
  Hawthorn Bush · *108*
  The Dog Inn · *108*
  The Gate · *108*
Sutton Mill · *89, 92*
Sutton-in-Craven · *88*

T

T. & M. Bairstow Ltd · *90, 91, 92, 93*
Tatler
  Denis Harold · *135, 137–39*
  Margaret S · *135, 137–39*
Taylor
  Marjorie Ann · *84*
  Rev John William Augustus · *14*
The Abbey Tearooms · *125*
The Bay Tree Hotel · *124*
The Blue Bird Tea Rooms · *125*
The Clans Private Hotel · *13, 21, 23*
The County Hotel · *94*
The Henburys · *27, 28, 29, 30, 31, 38, 42, 43, 45, 47*
The Monument · *33*
The Precinct of the Savoy' · *75*
The Priory' · *11*
The Sherington Hotel · *113, 124*
Thornham, Kings Lynn · *64, 65*
Thorp Arch Grange School · *87, 88*
Thorpe House · *13, 14, 19, 25, 26, 36, 145*

Tower House · *13, 15, 17, 137, 138, 139, 140, 141, 142, 143, 144*
Trail
  Margaret · *106, 107*
Tynemouth · *109, 110*

V

Valetta Hospital, Malta · *80*
van Wart
  Margaret Irving · *79, 81*

W

Wall nr Lichfield
  The Trooper · *108*
Ward
  C · *140*
Warner
  Flight Lt. Robert J. · *83*
Washwood Heath
  The Swan · *108*
Webster
  Dr John William England · *129*
  Joyce Margaret · *See* Sutcliffe Joyce Margaret
  Margaret · *129*
Wellingtonia · *See* Sequoia Dendron Gigantean
West
  Dr William Corner · *41, 42, 46, 54*
Wharry
  Arthur James · *71*
  Lily Adeline · *See* Barker Lily Adeline
Wharton
  Elizabeth · *See* Ratheram Elizabeth
  Thomas · *28, 31*
Whitworth

173

Colonel George · *125, 132*
Wighill · *87, 88, 91*
Wilcox
    Jack · 125, *132*
Willetts
    Alice Annie · *108*
    Esme Maud · *107–15*
    Evelyn Mabel · *109*
    John · *108*
    Martha · *108*
    Reuben · *108*
    Reuben William · *107, 108, 110*
    Thomas · *108*
    Thomas Dudley · *109*
    Walter · *109*
William Canning Ltd · *32, 33*

Williams
    Roy · *133, 134*
Wilson
    Dr James · *6, 94, 150*
Wilton
    Joseph · *14*
Winstanley, · *19, 21, 130*
Winter Gardens · *11*
Worcester Country Cricket Club · *81*

Y

Yates
    Hannah · *108*